President and Publisher
Ira Shapiro

Vice President Sales and Marketing
Marie-Christine Matter

Vice President Operations
Wendl Kornfeld

Production Director
Karen M. Bochow

Marketing Director
Ann Middlebrook

Marketing
Promotion/New Projects Manager
Stephanie Whitney
Marketing Coordinator
Lisa Wilker
Book Sales Coordinator
Cynthia Breneman

Advertising Sales
Sales Representatives:
John Bergstrom
Kate Hoffman
Ellen Kasemeier
Barbara Preminger
Joe Safferson
Wendy Saunders
Dave Tabler

Administration
Controller
Joel Kopel
Executive Assistant
Connie Grunwald
Accounting Assistant
Susan Su
Administrative Assistant
Paula Cohen

Published by:
American Showcase, Inc.
724 Fifth Avenue, 10th Floor
New York, New York 10019-4182
(212) 245-0981
FAX: (212) 265-2247
Telex: 880356 AMSHOW P

American Illustration
Showcase 13 Book 1of 2
ISBN 0-931144-61-2
ISSN 0278-8128

Cover Credits:
Front Cover Illustration:
Michael Schwab
Lead Page Illustration:
Marvin Mattelson

Production
Production Manager
Chuck Rosenow
Production Administrators:
Diane Cerafici
Tracy Russek
Traffic Coordinator
Stokes Hagg

Grey Pages
Distribution Manager
Scott Holden

Special Thanks to:
Ron Canagata
Amie Cooper
Julia Curry
Michael Joseph
Kyla Kanz
Fiona L'Estrange
Tina McKenna
Annie Newhall
Melissa Roldan
Joe Scala
Carol Schultz
Adam Seifer
Courtney Shapiro
Sandra Sierra
John Towey
Henrietta Valor

U.S. Book Trade Distribution:
Watson-Guptill Publications
1515 Broadway
New York, New York 10036
(212) 764-7300

For Sales outside the U.S.:
Rotovision S.A.
9 Route Suisse
1295 Mies, Switzerland
Telephone 022-735-3055
Telex 419246 ROVI

Book and Package Design:
Michael Peters Group

Mechanical Production:
American Showcase, Inc.

Typesetting:
**Ultra Typographic
Services, Inc.**

Color Separation, Printing and
Binding:
Dai Nippon Printing Co., LTD.

© 1990 American Showcase, Inc.
All rights reserved

**We're especially grateful to
Julia Martin Morris
for her ten years of
contribution to the growth
and success of
American Showcase.**

ILLUSTRATION 1 OF 2

AMERICAN
SHOWCASE

CONTENTS

V I E W P O I N T S

G R A P H I C   A R T S
O R G A N I Z A T I O N S

G R E Y   P A G E S

I N D E X

MAKE THE BEST ADDRESSED LIST WITH

REPRESENTATIVES

R
E
P
R
E
S
E
N
T
A
T
I
V
E
S

REPRESENTATIVES

BERNSTEIN & ANDRIULLI
REPRESENTATIVES

BERNSTEIN & ANDRIULLI INC, 60 EAST 42ND STREET, NEW YORK, NY 10165, FAX (212) 286-1890 **(212) 682-1490**

REPRESENTATIVES

BERNSTEIN & ANDRIULLI INC, 60 EAST 42ND STREET, NEW YORK, NY 10165, FAX (212) 286-1890 **(212) 682-1490**

REPRESENTATIVES

BERNSTEIN & ANDRIULLI INC, 60 EAST 42ND STREET, NEW YORK, NY 10165, FAX (212) 286-1890 **(212) 682-1490**

D A N I E L   C R A I G

REPRESENTATIVES

BERNSTEIN & ANDRIULLI INC, 60 EAST 42ND STREET, NEW YORK, NY 10165, FAX (212) 286-1890 **(212) 682-1490**

EVERETT DAVIDSON

BERNSTEIN & ANDRIULLI

REPRESENTATIVES

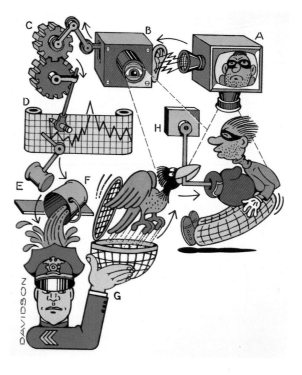

BERNSTEIN & ANDRIULLI INC, 60 EAST 42ND STREET, NEW YORK, NY 10165, FAX (212) 286-1890 **(212) 682-1490**

NINA DURAN

REPRESENTATIVES

BERNSTEIN & ANDRIULLI INC, 60 EAST 42ND STREET, NEW YORK, NY 10165, FAX (212) 286-1890 **(212) 682-1490**

RON FLEMING

REPRESENTATIVES

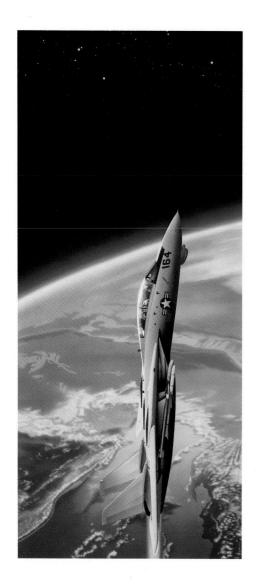

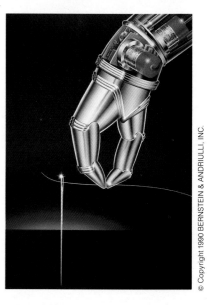

BERNSTEIN & ANDRIULLI INC, 60 EAST 42ND STREET, NEW YORK, NY 10165, FAX (212) 286-1890 **(212) 682-1490**

REPRESENTATIVES

© 1989 Lucasfilm Ltd.

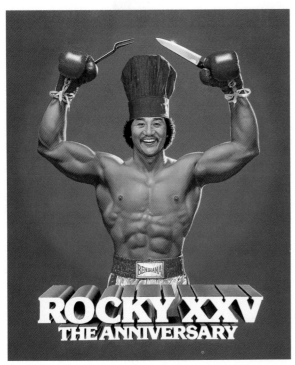

BERNSTEIN & ANDRIULLI INC, 60 EAST 42ND STREET, NEW YORK, NY 10165, FAX (212) 286-1890 **(212) 682-1490**

JOE GENOVA

REPRESENTATIVES

BERNSTEIN & ANDRIULLI INC, 60 EAST 42ND STREET, NEW YORK, NY 10165, FAX (212) 286-1890 **(212) 682-1490**

REPRESENTATIVES

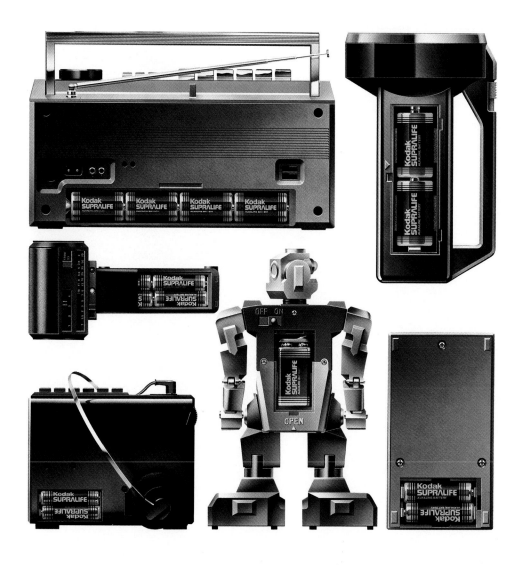

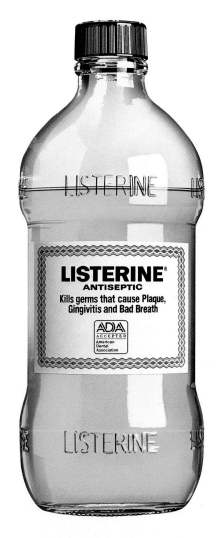

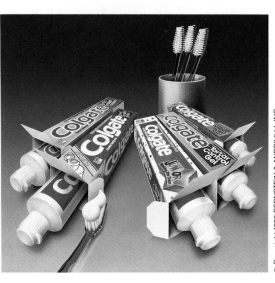

BERNSTEIN & ANDRIULLI INC, 60 EAST 42ND STREET, NEW YORK, NY 10165, FAX (212) 286-1890 **(212) 682-1490**

TIM JESSELL

REPRESENTATIVES

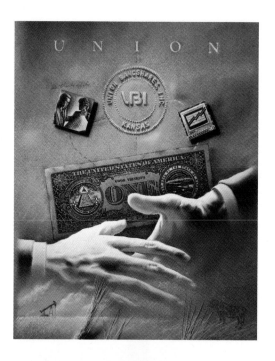

BERNSTEIN & ANDRIULLI INC, 60 EAST 42ND STREET, NEW YORK, NY 10165, FAX (212) 286-1890 **(212) 682-1490**

MARY ANN LASHER

REPRESENTATIVES

BERNSTEIN & ANDRIULLI INC, 60 EAST 42ND STREET, NEW YORK, NY 10165, FAX (212) 286-1890 **(212) 682-1490**

BETTE LEVINE

REPRESENTATIVES

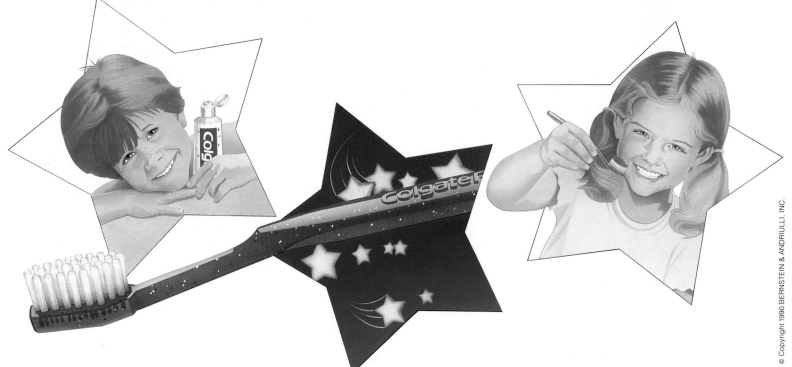

BERNSTEIN & ANDRIULLI INC, 60 EAST 42ND STREET, NEW YORK, NY 10165, FAX (212) 286-1890 **(212) 682-1490**

TODD LOCKWOOD

REPRESENTATIVES

BERNSTEIN & ANDRIULLI INC, 60 EAST 42ND STREET, NEW YORK, NY 10165, FAX (212) 286-1890 **(212) 682-1490**

LEE MᵃcLEOD

REPRESENTATIVES

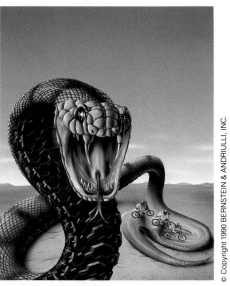

BERNSTEIN & ANDRIULLI INC, 60 EAST 42ND STREET, NEW YORK, NY 10165, FAX (212) 286-1890 **(212) 682-1490**

DAVID B. McMACKEN

REPRESENTATIVES

BERNSTEIN & ANDRIULLI INC, 60 EAST 42ND STREET, NEW YORK, NY 10165, FAX (212) 286-1890 **(212) 682-1490**

CHRIS MOORE

BERNSTEIN&
ANDRIULLI

REPRESENTATIVES

BERNSTEIN & ANDRIULLI INC, 60 EAST 42ND STREET, NEW YORK, NY 10165, FAX (212) 286-1890 **(212) 682-1490**

CRAIG NELSON

REPRESENTATIVES

BERNSTEIN & ANDRIULLI INC, 60 EAST 42ND STREET, NEW YORK, NY 10165, FAX (212) 286-1890 **(212) 682-1490**

JEFF NISHINAKA

REPRESENTATIVES

BERNSTEIN & ANDRIULLI INC, 60 EAST 42ND STREET, NEW YORK, NY 10165, FAX (212) 286-1890 **(212) 682-1490**

REPRESENTATIVES

BERNSTEIN & ANDRIULLI INC, 60 EAST 42ND STREET, NEW YORK, NY 10165, FAX (212) 286-1890 **(212) 682-1490**

PEGGI ROBERTS

REPRESENTATIVES

BERNSTEIN & ANDRIULLI INC, 60 EAST 42ND STREET, NEW YORK, NY 10165, FAX (212) 286-1890 **(212) 682-1490**

RAY ROBERTS

REPRESENTATIVES

BERNSTEIN & ANDRIULLI INC, 60 EAST 42ND STREET, NEW YORK, NY 10165, FAX (212) 286-1890 **(212) 682-1490**

BERNSTEIN & ANDRIULLI

REPRESENTATIVES

BERNSTEIN & ANDRIULLI INC, 60 EAST 42ND STREET, NEW YORK, NY 10165, FAX (212) 286-1890 **(212) 682-1490**

REPRESENTATIVES

BERNSTEIN & ANDRIULLI INC, 60 EAST 42ND STREET, NEW YORK, NY 10165, FAX (212) 286-1890 **(212) 682-1490**

REPRESENTATIVES

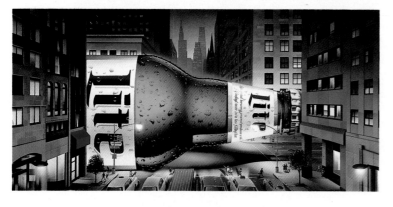

BERNSTEIN & ANDRIULLI INC, 60 EAST 42ND STREET, NEW YORK, NY 10165, FAX (212) 286-1890 **(212) 682-1490**

REPRESENTATIVES

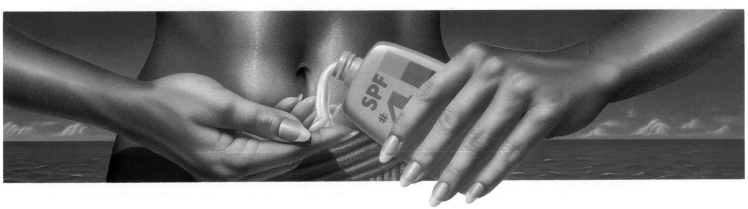

BERNSTEIN & ANDRIULLI INC, 60 EAST 42ND STREET, NEW YORK, NY 10165, FAX (212) 286-1890 **(212) 682-1490**

BRENT WATKINSON

REPRESENTATIVES

BERNSTEIN & ANDRIULLI INC, 60 EAST 42ND STREET, NEW YORK, NY 10165, FAX (212) 286-1890 **(212) 682-1490**

REPRESENTATIVES

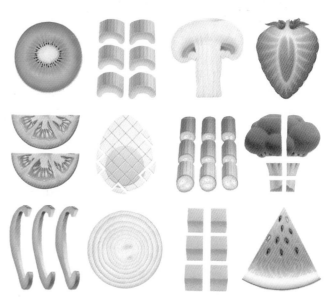

BERNSTEIN & ANDRIULLI INC, 60 EAST 42ND STREET, NEW YORK, NY 10165, FAX (212) 286-1890 **(212) 682-1490**

Renard Represents

JÖZEF SUMICHRAST

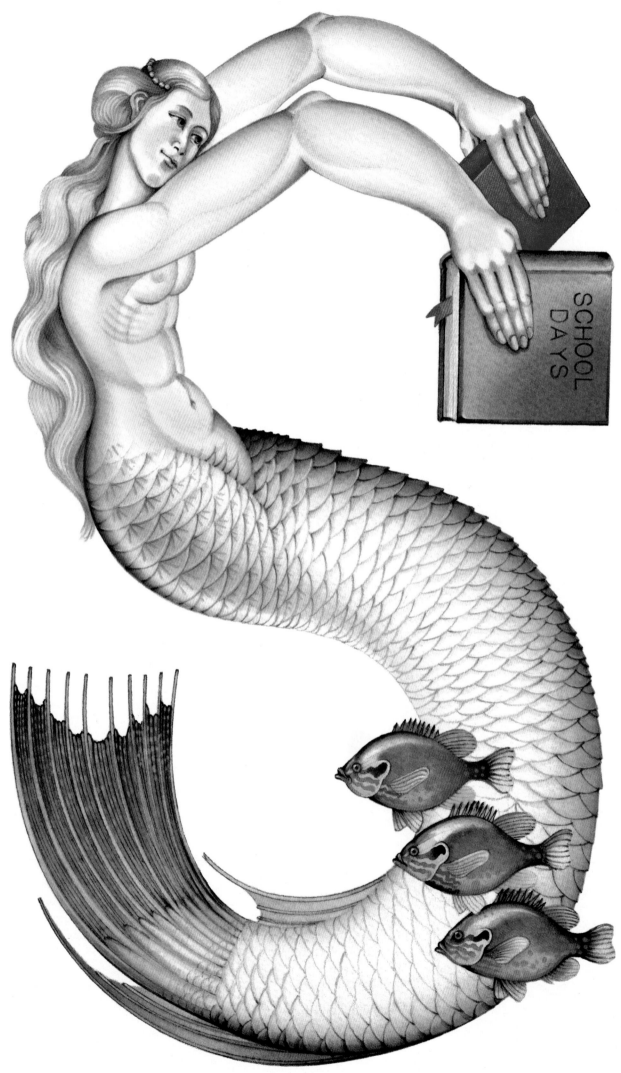

Renard Represents Inc.
501 Fifth Avenue
New York, N.Y. 10017
Tel: 212 490 2450
Fax: 212 697 6828

Renard Represents

BART FORBES

America the Beautiful USA **15**

Renard Represents Inc.
501 Fifth Avenue
New York, NY 10017
Tel (212) 490 2450
Fax (212) 697 6828

Renard Represents

RICHARD NEWTON

Renard Represents Inc.
501 Fifth Avenue
New York, NY 10017
Tel (212) 490 2450
Fax (212) 697 6828

Renard Represents

KIM
WHITESIDES

Renard Represents Inc.
501 Fifth Avenue
New York, N.Y. 10017
Tel: 212 490 2450
Fax: 212 697 6828

FLORIDA NATIONAL JAZZ FESTIVAL
JACKSONVILLE '88

49

Renard Represents

JOHN
MARTIN

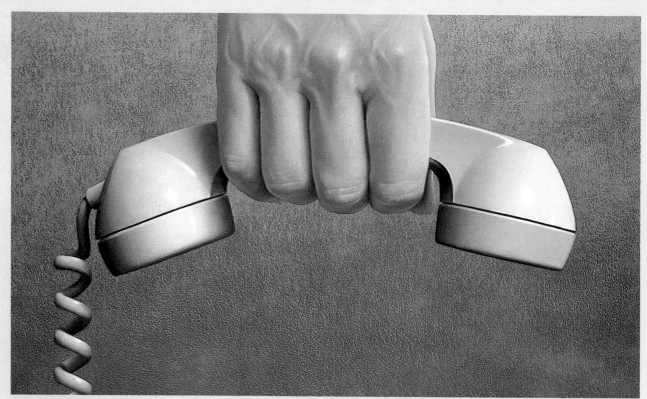

Renard Represents Inc.
501 Fifth Avenue
New York, NY 10017
Tel (212) 490 2450
Fax (212) 697 6828

Renard Represents

ROBERT
RODRIGUEZ

Renard Represents Inc.
501 Fifth Avenue
New York, NY 10017
Tel (212) 490 2450
Fax (212) 697 6828

© 1990 STEVE BJÖRKMAN

Renard Represents

ROB DAY

NICOLAS · JENSON

Renard Represents Inc.
501 Fifth Avenue
New York, NY 10017
Tel (212) 490 2450
Fax (212) 697 6828

Renard Represents

DOUG STRUTHERS

Doug Struthers' imagery can be reproduced as a 3D stereo give-away viewer. Easily combined with product photography or illustration to give direct mail or trade shows unforgettable impact. Call for a free sample.

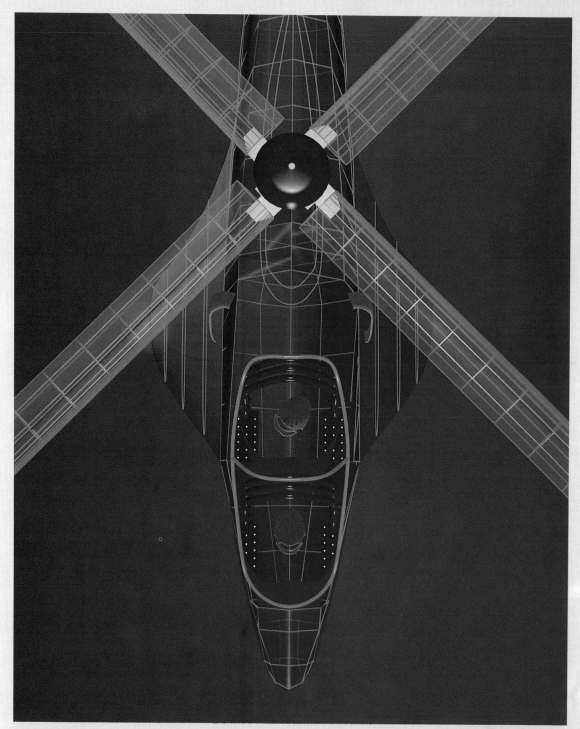

Renard Represents Inc.
501 Fifth Avenue
New York, NY 10017
Tel (212) 490 2450
Fax (212) 697 6828

© 1990 DOUG STRUTHERS

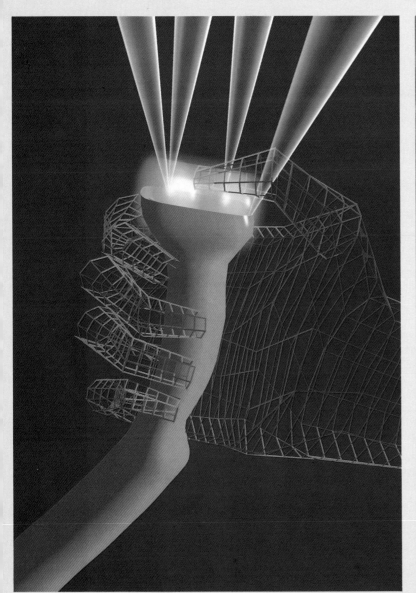

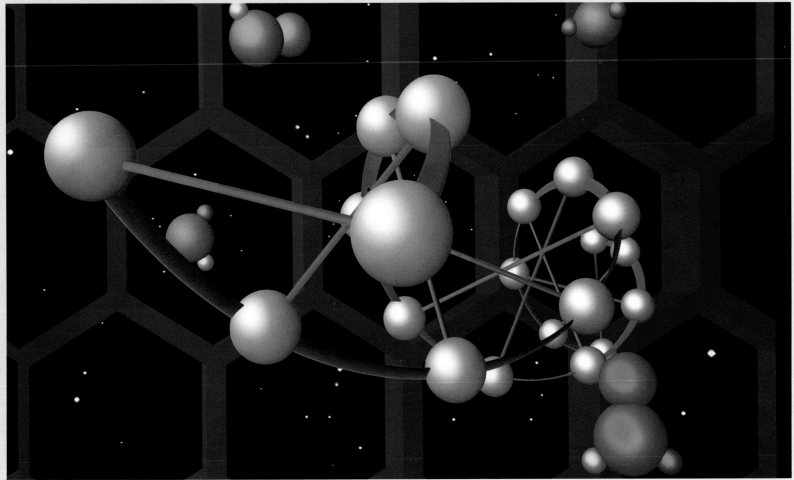

Renard Represents

CAROL
DONNER

Medical and Conceptual
Illustration

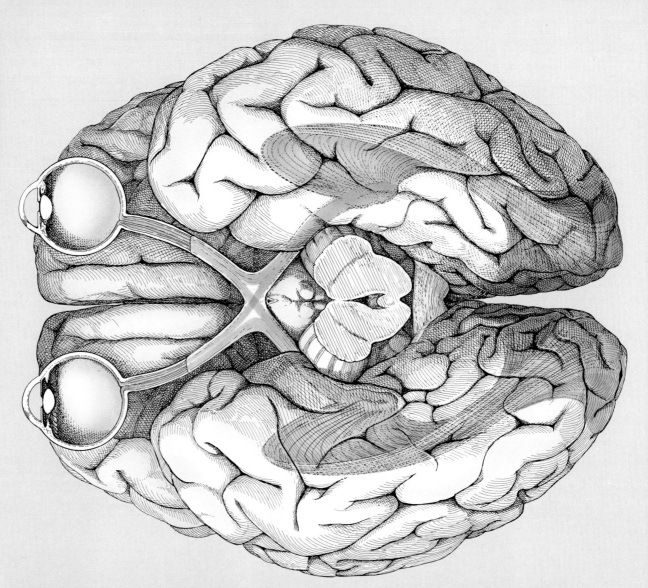

Renard Represents Inc.
501 Fifth Avenue
New York, NY 10017
Tel (212) 490 2450
Fax (212) 697 6828

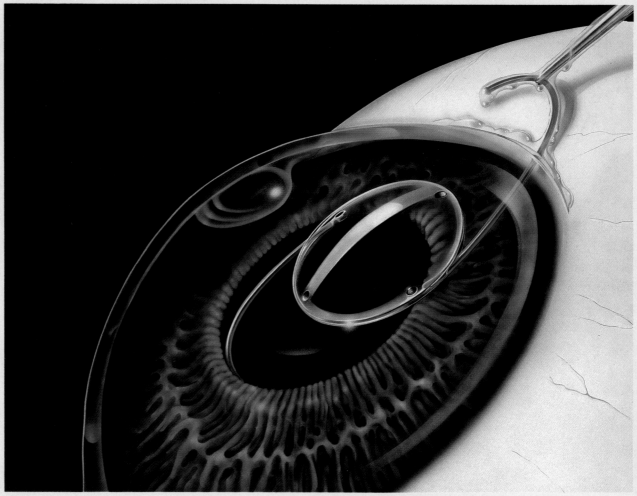

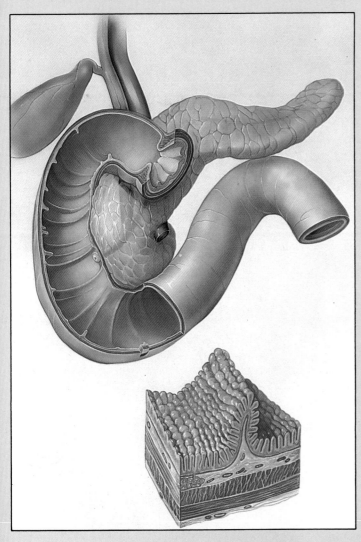

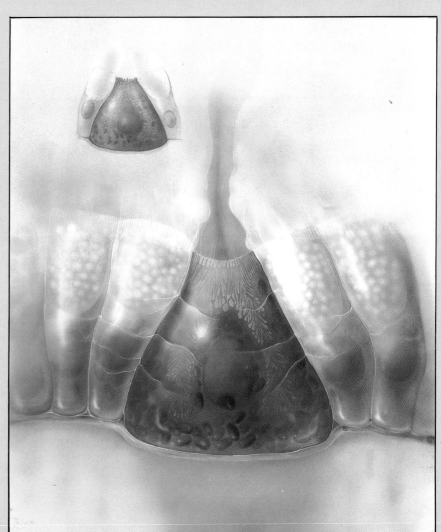

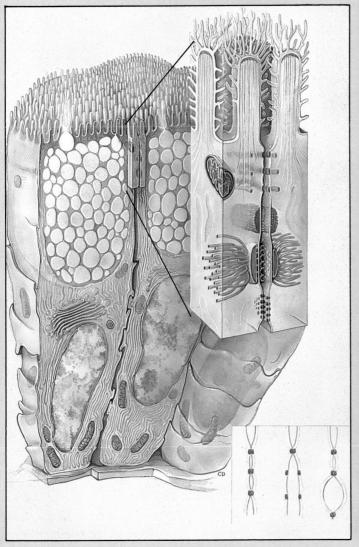

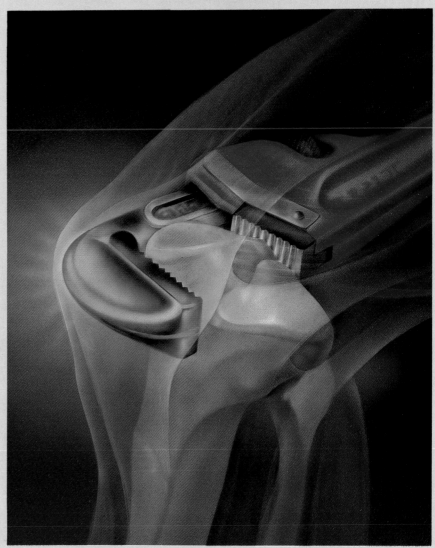

Renard Represents

in association with:

Personality Inc.
2-12-35, Minamikaneden
Suitashi, Osaka 564 Japan
Tel: 06-386-6921
Fax: 06-386-6560
Tlx: J64483 NIPOSTER
Tokyo Tel: 03-464-3241

SAITO

KODAMA

SHIMAOKA

In U.S. and Canada contact:

Renard Represents Inc.
501 Fifth Avenue
New York, N.Y. 10017
Tel: 212 490 2450
Fax: 212 697 6828

© 1990 HIDEAKI KODAMA

© 1990 GORO SHIMAOKA

JOHN HOLM

GARY CICCARELLI

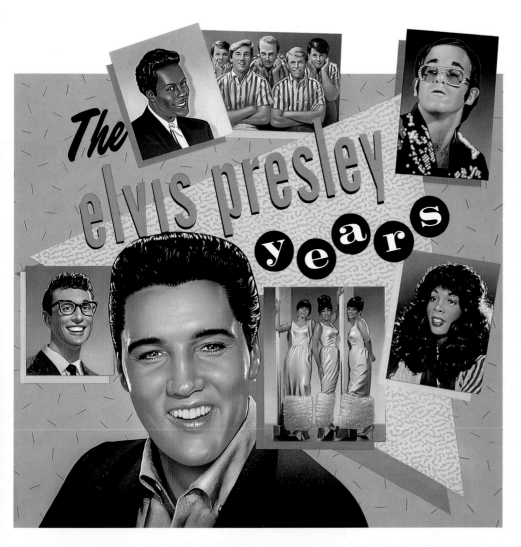

ALAN LEINER

SEE ADDITIONAL WORK IN CREATIVE ILLUSTRATION BOOK #1

MICHAEL ELINS

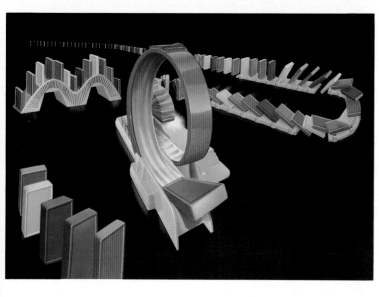

MALCOLM FARLEY

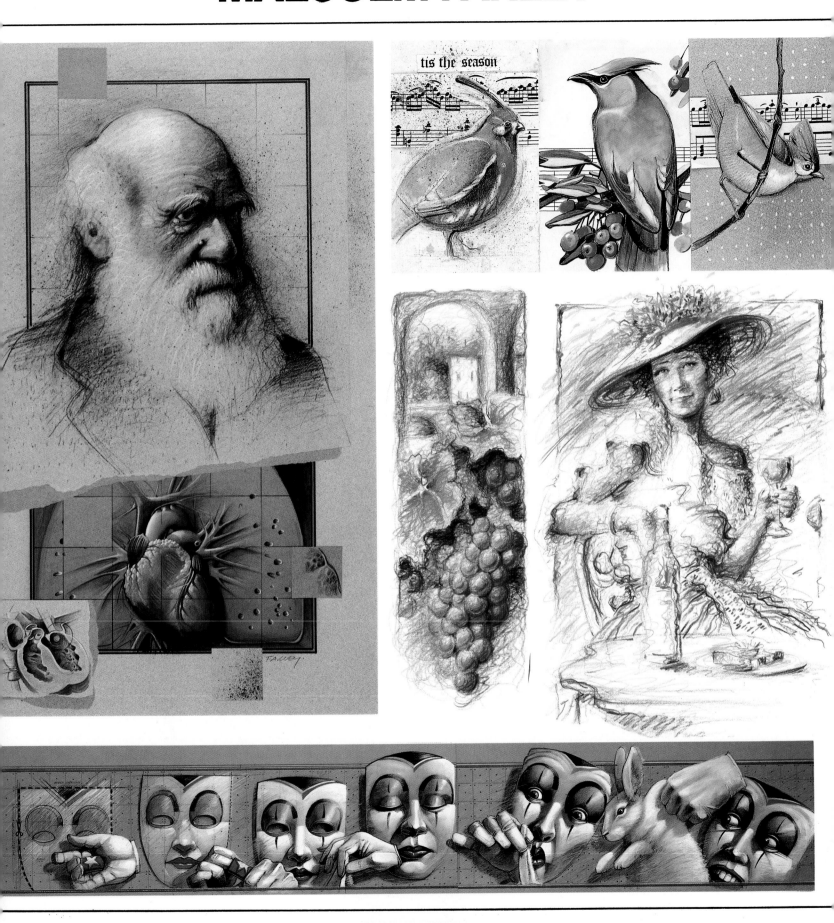

MITCH HYATT

JOSEPH SCROFANI

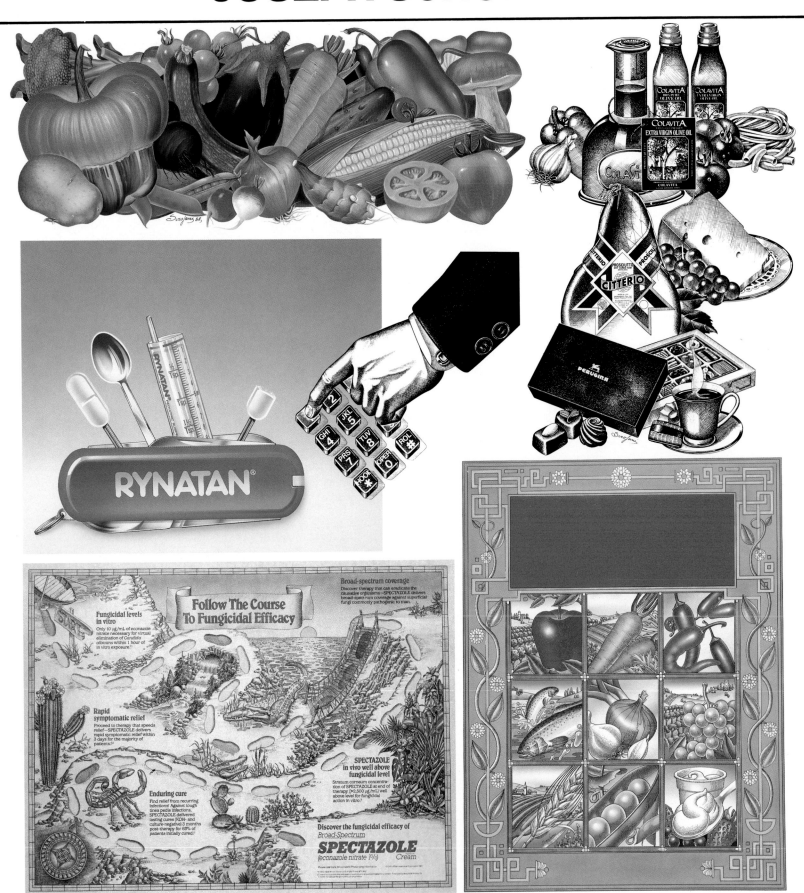

JEAN-CLAUDE MICHEL

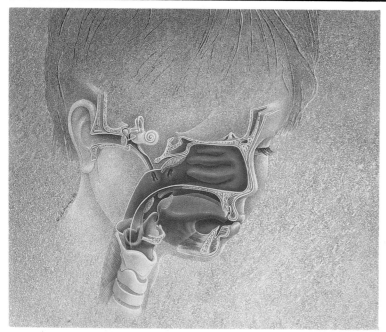

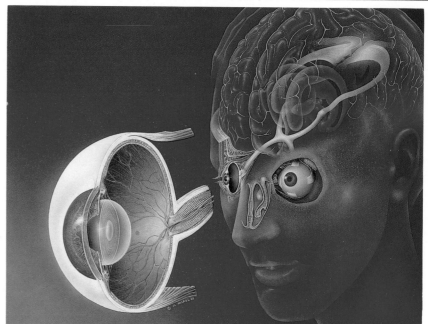

GARY YEALDHALL

The JiffyLube GRAND SLAM GIVEAWAY

· ORIOLES · BASEBALL ·
· APRIL · OCTOBER ·
· MEMORIAL STADIUM ·

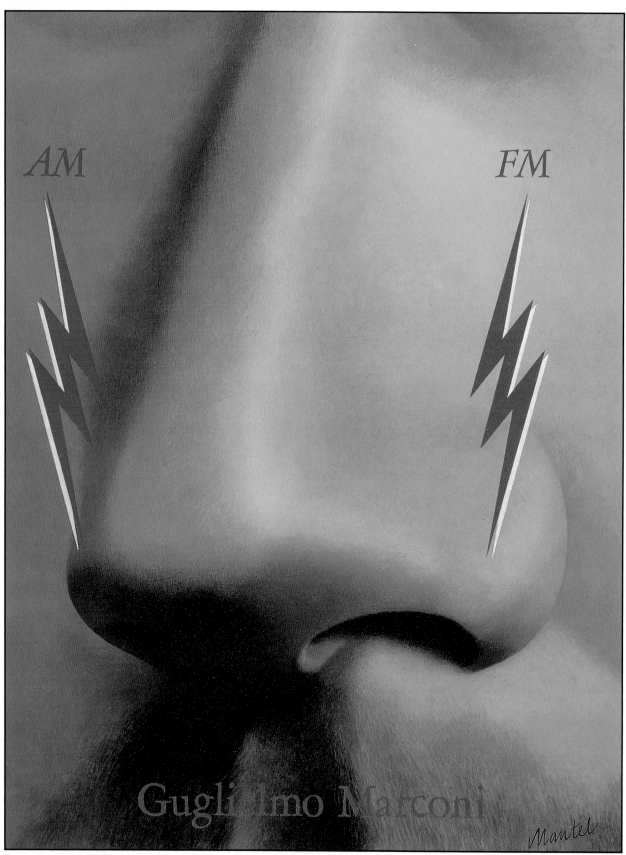

TRATTORIA DEL ARTE

OUTSIDE THE NORTHEAST CALL JAN COLLIER 415-552-4252

212-929-5590

WARREN EVERETT QUIST ATTEMPTS TO LEAP INTO ANOTHER GLASS OF WATER

A BAD DAY IN THE LIFE OF THE FIREPROOF WOMAN.

MRS. SIMPSON'S 2ⁿᵈ GRADE CLASS REENACTS THE MURDER OF LEE H. OSWALD

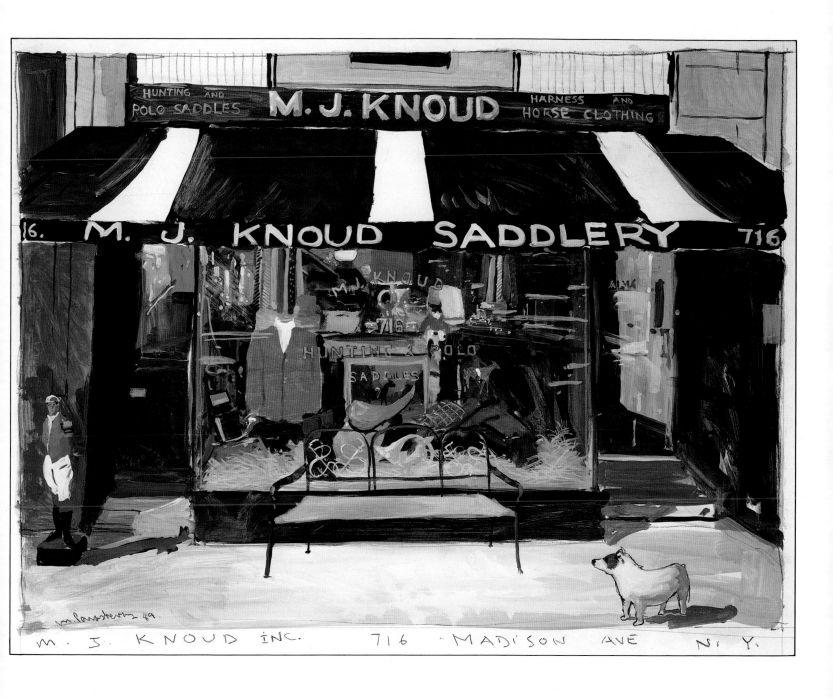

JEAN WISENBAUGH

CHARTS
MAPS
DIAGRAMS

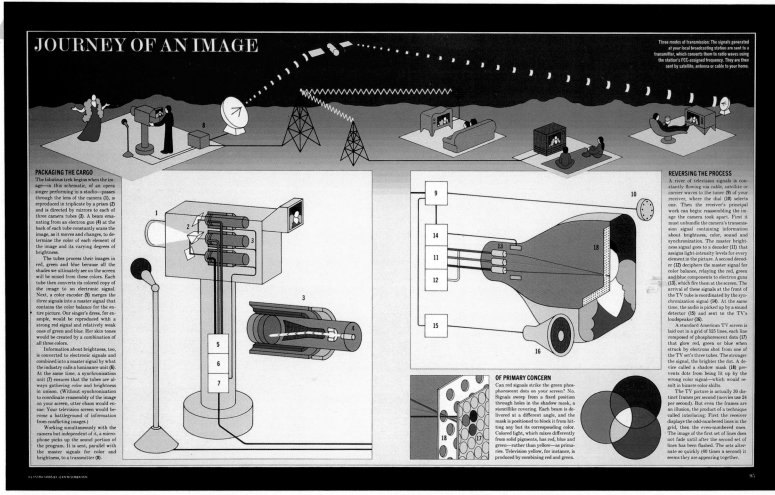

JOURNEY OF AN IMAGE

Three modes of transmission: The signals generated at your local broadcasting station are sent to a transmitter, which converts them to radio waves using the station's FCC-assigned frequency. They are then sent by satellite, antenna or cable to your home.

PACKAGING THE CARGO

The fabulous trek begins when the image—in this schematic, of an opera singer performing in a studio—passes through the lens of the camera (1), is reproduced in triplicate by a prism (2) and is directed by mirrors to each of three camera tubes (3). A beam emanating from an electron gun (4) at the back of each tube constantly scans the image, as it moves and changes, to determine the color of each element of the image and its varying degrees of brightness.

The tubes process their images in red, green and blue because all the shades we ultimately see on the screen will be mixed from these colors. Each tube then converts its colored copy of the image to an electronic signal. Next, a color encoder (5) merges the three signals into a master signal that contains the color balance for the entire picture. Our singer's dress, for example, would be reproduced with a strong red signal and relatively weak ones of green and blue. Her skin tones would be created by a combination of all three colors.

Information about brightness, too, is converted to electronic signals and combined into a master signal by what the industry calls a luminance unit (6). At the same time, a synchronization unit (7) ensures that the tubes are always gathering color and brightness in unison. (Without synchronization to coordinate reassembly of the image on your screen, utter chaos would ensue: Your television screen would become a battleground of information from conflicting images.)

Working simultaneously with the camera but independent of it, a microphone picks up the sound portion of the program. It is sent, parallel with the master signals for color and brightness, to a transmitter (8).

OF PRIMARY CONCERN

Can red signals strike the green phosphorescent dots on your screen? No. Signals sweep from a fixed position through holes in the shadow mask, a stencillike covering. Each beam is delivered at a different angle, and the mask is positioned to block it from hitting any but its corresponding color. Colored light, which mixes differently from solid pigments, has red, blue and green—rather than yellow—as primaries. Television yellow, for instance, is produced by combining red and green.

REVERSING THE PROCESS

A river of television signals is constantly flowing via cable, satellite or carrier waves to the tuner (9) of your receiver, where the dial (10) selects one. Then the receiver's principal work can begin: reassembling the image the camera took apart. First it must unbundle the camera's transmission signal containing information about brightness, color, sound and synchronization. The master brightness signal goes to a decoder (11) that assigns light-intensity levels for every element in the picture. A second decoder (12) deciphers the master signal for color balance, relaying the red, green and blue components to electron guns (13), which fire them at the screen. The arrival of these signals at the front of the TV tube is coordinated by the synchronization signal (14). At the same time, the audio is picked up by a sound detector (15) and sent to the TV's loudspeaker (16).

A standard American TV screen is laid out in a grid of 525 lines, each line composed of phosphorescent dots (17) that glow red, green or blue when struck by electrons shot from one of the TV set's three tubes. The stronger the signal, the brighter the dot. A device called a shadow mask (18) prevents dots from being lit up by the wrong color signal—which would result in bizarre color shifts.

The TV picture is actually 30 distinct frames per second (movies use 24 per second). But even the frames are an illusion, the product of a technique called interlacing: First the receiver displays the odd-numbered lines in the grid, then the even-numbered ones. The image of the first set of lines does not fade until after the second set of lines has been flashed. The sets alternate so quickly (60 times a second) it seems they are appearing together.

ILLUSTRATIONS BY JEAN WISENBAUGH

95

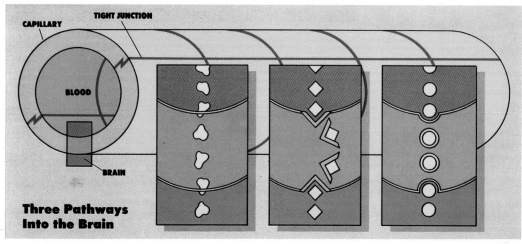

CAPILLARY

TIGHT JUNCTION

BLOOD

BRAIN

Three Pathways Into the Brain

BARBARA BANTHIEN

DARRYL ZUDECK

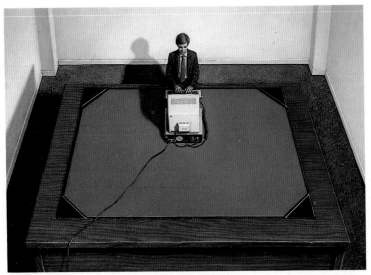

PC MAGAZINE

RANDOM HOUSE

HARPER & ROW

ST. MARTIN'S PRESS

ALSO SEE: SOCIETY OF ILLUSTRATORS ANNUAL 26 THROUGH 30, AMERICAN ILLUSTRATION NO. 2,
OUTSTANDING AMERICAN ILLUSTRATION NO. 2, AMERICAN SHOWCASE NO. 12.

OUTSIDE THE NORTHEAST CALL JAN COLLIER 415-552-4252

KATHY O'BRIEN

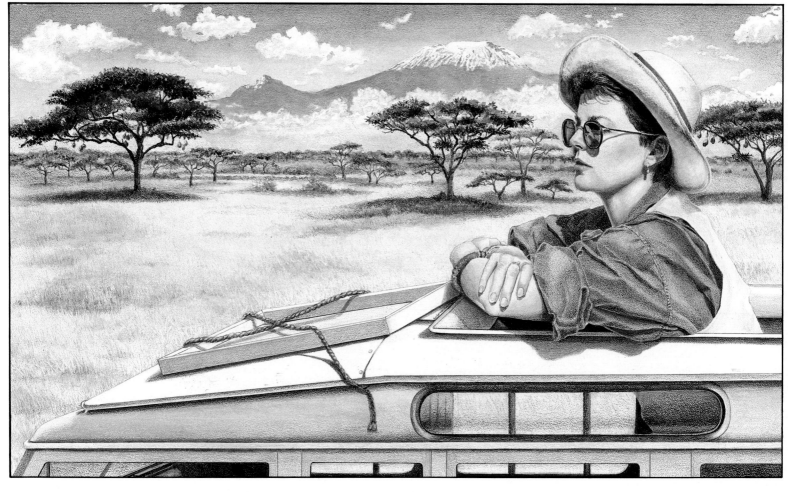

TIM RAGLIN

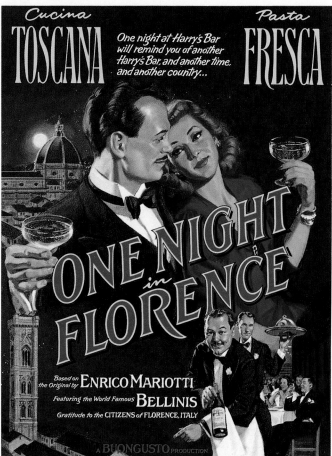

JACQUELINE DEDELL, INC.

Artist Representative

REPRESENTING

Cathie Bleck

Ivan Chermayeff

Teresa Fasolino

David Frampton

Cheryl Griesbach/Stanley Martucci

Paula Munck

Edward Parker

Keith Richens

Barrett Root

Kimberly Bulcken Root

Isadore Seltzer

Richard Williams

Chermayeff & Geismar Associates

Jacqueline Dedell, Inc.
58 West 15th Street
New York, New York 10011
Tel: (212) 741-2539
Fax: (212) 741-4660

JACQUELINE DEDELL, INC.

Jacqueline Dedell, Inc.

58 West 15th Street
New York, New York, 10011
Tel: (212) 741-2539

Representing
GRIESBACH/MARTUCCI

Chief Executive

Lardis, McCurdy & Co.

Avon Books

PC Resource

Ballantine

Backer Spielvogel Bates

Al Paul Lefton

Jacqueline Dedell, Inc.

58 West 15th Street
New York, New York, 10011
Tel: (212) 741-2539

Representing

CATHIE BLECK

Business Week

New York Times

Outside Magazine

Samata Design

Business Monthly

Michael Peters Group

JACQUELINE DEDELL, INC.

CB

Jacqueline Dedell, Inc.

58 West 15th Street
New York, New York, 10011
Tel: (212) 741-2539

Representing
TERESA FASOLINO

Backer Spielvogel Bates

IBM

Martin Agency

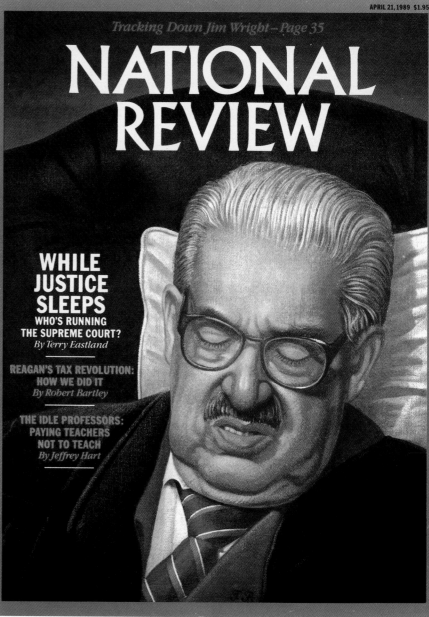

Pentagram Design

Prentice Hall

Workman Publishing

Cochrane, Chase, Livingston & Co.

Jacqueline Dedell, Inc.

58 West 15th Street
New York, New York, 10011
Tel: (212) 741-2539
Representing
RICHARD WILLIAMS

Della Femina McNamee WCRS

Canard Design

Little Brown & Co.

Della Femina McNamee WCRS

Canard Design

Reader's Digest

JACQUELINE DEDELL, INC.

Jacqueline Dedell, Inc.

58 West 15th Street
New York, New York 10011
Tel: (212) 741-2539

Representing
PAULA MUNCK

Body Shop

Goodlife Magazine

EN PROVENCE

Ann Waldman Associates

Boston Globe

Jacqueline Dedell, Inc.

58 West 15th Street
New York, New York, 10011
Tel: (212) 741-2539

Representing

EDWARD PARKER

McCall's

Rosin, Greenberg, Seronick & Hill

Downeast Design

Leonard, Lubars & Partners

Equestrian Shop

McCall's

Village Landscaping

Mitchell Hooks

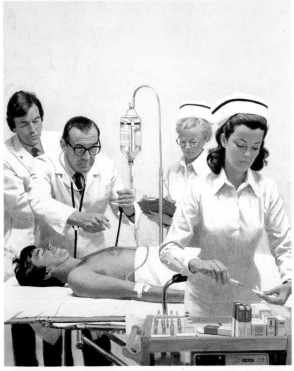

Mitchell Hooks

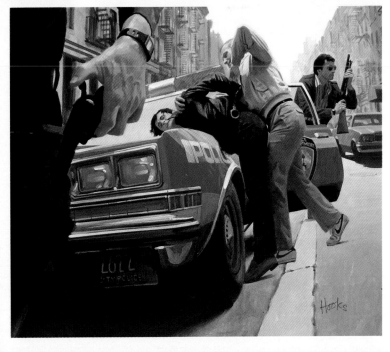

Puts colour
in your cheeks.

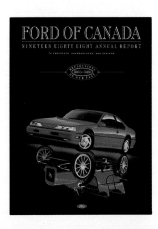

FORD OF CANADA

NINETEEN EIGHTY EIGHT ANNUAL REPORT

HOMPSON

BFGOODRICH T/A RADIALS

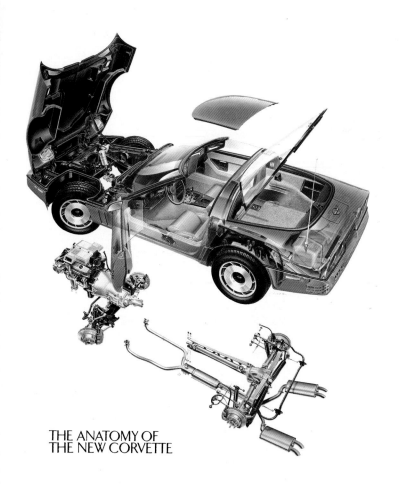

THE ANATOMY OF
THE NEW CORVETTE

RICHARD LEECH

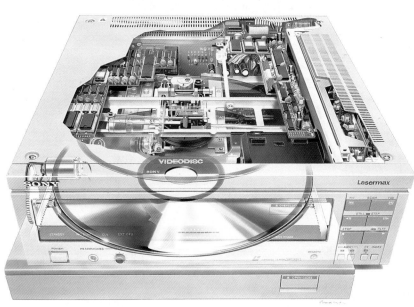

KIP SOLDWEDEL

CHRIS

NOTARILE

STEVE BRENNAN

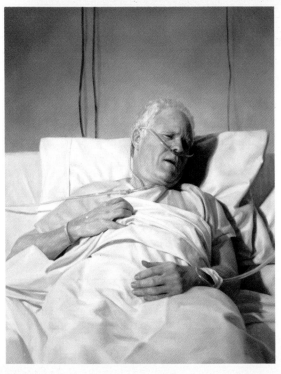

(212)
986-5680
FAX NO.
(212) 818-1246

Mendola LTD.

GRAYBAR BLDG · 420 LEXINGTON AVE · PENTHOUSE · NEW YORK, NY 10170

ATTILA HEJJA

JOHN SOLIE

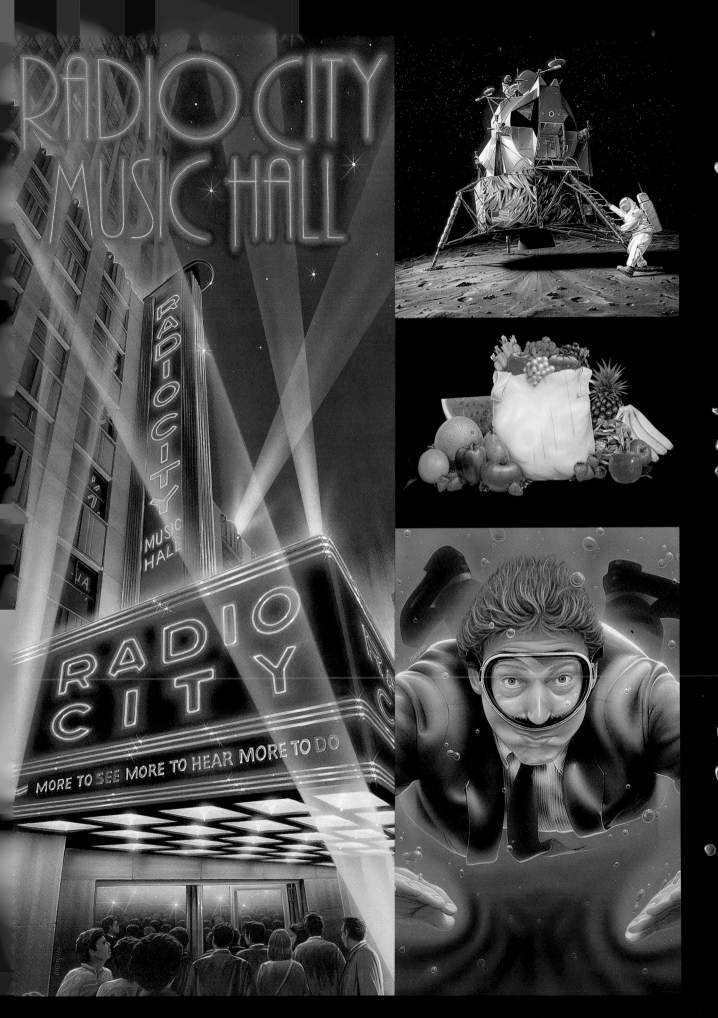

CARL CASSLER

MIKE WIMMER

JIM DENEEN

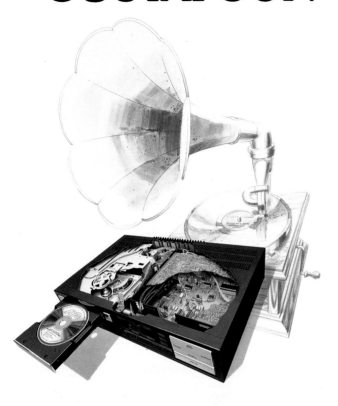
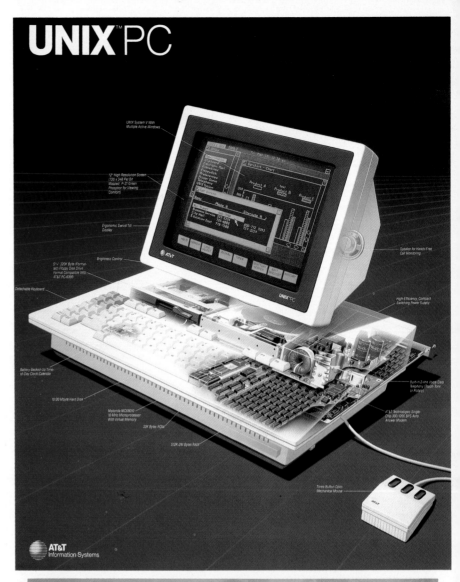

MARK · WATTS INC.

ILLUSTRATION · TYPE · DESIGN

Thunderbird

pink **Cadillac**

PHIL FRANKE

MICHAEL SMOLLIN

ALFONS
KIEFER

DENNIS LYALL

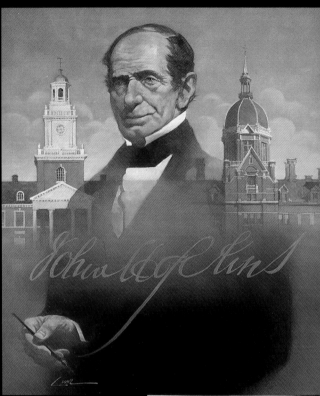

(212) 986-5680 FAX NO. (212) 818-1246

GRAYBAR BLDG. · 420 LEXINGTON AVE. · PENTHOUSE · NEW YORK, NY 10170

Mendola LTD.

MIKE MIKOS

(212) **986-5680** FAX NO. (212) 818-1246

Mendola LTD.

GRAYBAR BLDG · 420 LEXINGTON AVE · PENTHOUSE · NEW YORK NY 10170

JIM CAMPBELL

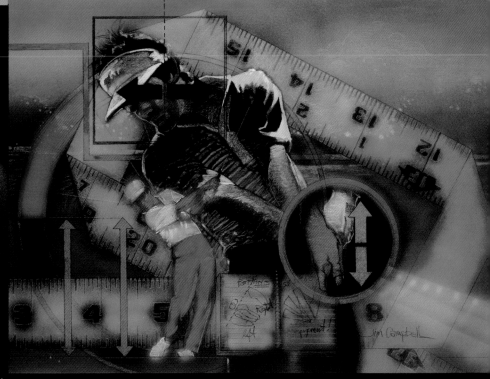

GEOFF McCORMACK

DELRO ROSCO

EDWARD MARTINEZ

DEBORAH L. CHABRIAN

JON ELLIS

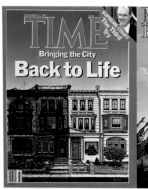

DAVID SCHLEINKOFER

(212) **986-5680** FAX NO. (212) 818-1246

Mendola LTD.

JOHN EGGERT

DAVID HENDERSON

BRIAN SAURIOL

5
FLEET
DISTRIBUTOR

(212) 986-5680 FAX NO. (212) 818-1246

Mendola LTD.

GRAYBAR BLDG · 420 LEXINGTON AVE · PENTHOUSE · NEW YORK, NY 10170

PAUL ALEXANDER

CATHY MORRIS, ASSOCIATE

RICHARD SOLOMON • ARTIST REPRESENTATIVE • 121 MADISON AVE. • NYC 10016 • (212) 683-1362 • FAX: (212) 683-1919

BURMA / PEN & COLOR INK

RICHARD SOLOMON ▪ ARTIST REPRESENTATIVE ▪ 121 MADISON AVE. ▪ NYC 10016 ▪ (212) 683-1362 ▪ FAX: (212) 683-1919

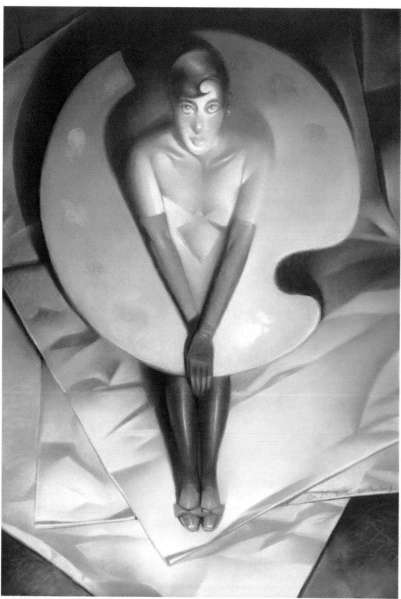

PERFORMANCE ARTIST / PASTEL

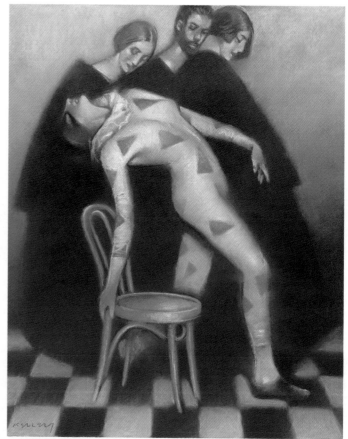

HARLEQUIN

LU HSUN, REVOLUTIONARY POET

MISSING LINK

RICHARD SOLOMON • ARTIST REPRESENTATIVE • 121 MADISON AVE. • NYC 10016 • (212) 683-1362 • FAX: (212) 683-1919

PICASSO'S PARTY / PASTEL

RICHARD SOLOMON ▪ ARTIST REPRESENTATIVE ▪ 121 MADISON AVE. ▪ NYC 10016 ▪ (212) 683-1362 ▪ FAX: (212) 683-1919

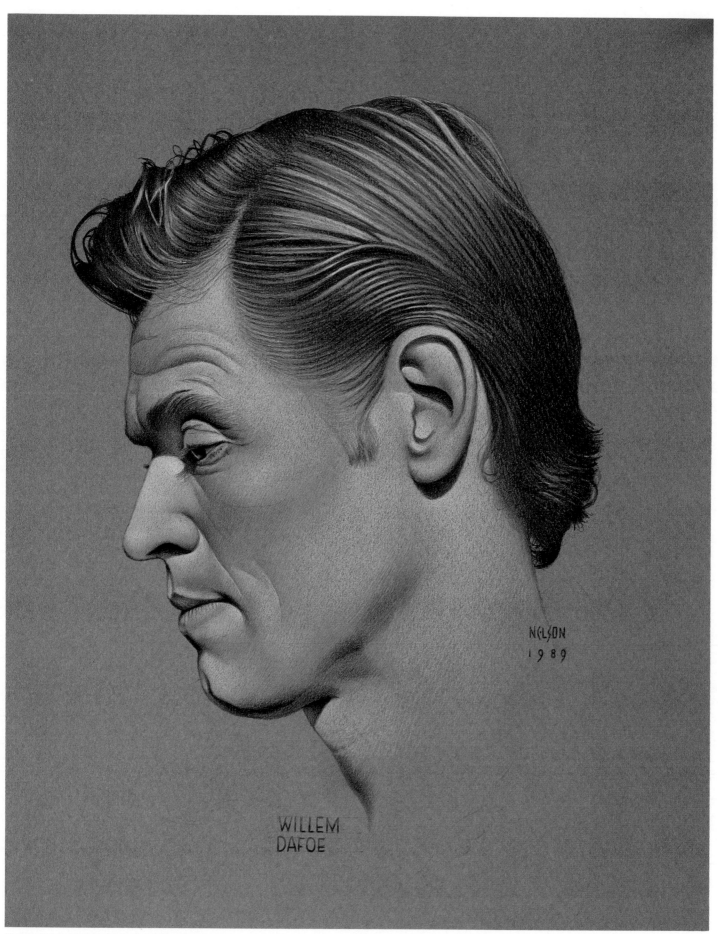

WILLEM DAFOE / COLORED PENCIL ON CANSON PAPER

RICHARD SOLOMON ▪ ARTIST REPRESENTATIVE ▪ 121 MADISON AVE. ▪ NYC 10016 ▪ (212) 683-1362 ▪ FAX: (212) 683-1919

STEP-BY-STEP / COLORED PENCIL ON CANSON PAPER

CHICAGO JAZZ / MIXED MEDIA

MOONLIGHT

LION IN ICE CAVERN

RICHARD SOLOMON • ARTIST REPRESENTATIVE • 121 MADISON AVE. • NYC 10016 • (212) 683-1362 • FAX: (212) 683-1919

THE WITNESS / MIXED MEDIA

RICHARD SOLOMON ▪ ARTIST REPRESENTATIVE ▪ 121 MADISON AVE. ▪ NYC 10016 ▪ (212) 683-1362 ▪ FAX: (212) 683-1919

QUIN SHIHUANG / PEN & INK

DUSTIN HOFFMAN IN <u>DEATH OF A SALESMAN</u>

JOHN CALVIN

TOM HANKS

NOMADS OF MALI / PEN & INK & WATERCOLOR

RICHARD SOLOMON ▪ ARTIST REPRESENTATIVE ▪ 121 MADISON AVE. ▪ NYC 10016 ▪ (212) 683-1362 ▪ FAX: (212) 683-1919

DOUGLAS SMITH

A BRITISH SHIP OF THE LINE, 1809 / SCRATCHBOARD & WATERCOLOR

RICHARD SOLOMON ▪ ARTIST REPRESENTATIVE ▪ 121 MADISON AVE. ▪ NYC 10016 ▪ (212) 683-1362 ▪ FAX: (212) 683-1919

DON QUIXOTE / SCRATCHBOARD

RICHARD SOLOMON ▪ ARTIST REPRESENTATIVE ▪ 121 MADISON AVE. ▪ NYC 10016 ▪ (212) 683-1362 ▪ FAX: (212) 683-1919

SIGMUND FREUD / SCRATCHBOARD

PRIVATE EYE

EUGENE O'NEILL

ORSON WELLES

PICKWICK PAPERS / SCRATCHBOARD & WATERCOLOR

RICHARD SOLOMON ▪ ARTIST REPRESENTATIVE ▪ 121 MADISON AVE. ▪ NYC 10016 ▪ (212) 683-1362 ▪ FAX: (212) 683-1919

CAPTAIN JACK CRAWFORD'S FRONTIER SCOUTS / SCRATCHBOARD & WATERCOLOR

RICHARD SOLOMON • ARTIST REPRESENTATIVE • 121 MADISON AVE. • NYC 10016 • (212) 683-1362 • FAX: (212) 683-1919

MICHELLE PFEIFFER / SCRATCHBOARD

HARRISON FORD

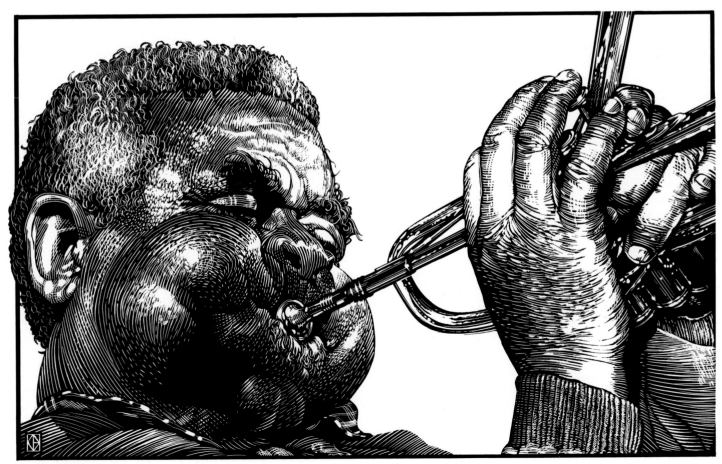

DIZZY GILLESPIE

RICHARD SOLOMON ▪ ARTIST REPRESENTATIVE ▪ 121 MADISON AVE. ▪ NYC 10016 ▪ (212) 683-1362 ▪ FAX: (212) 683-1919

LITTLE GEORGE FAUNTLEROY / MIXED MEDIA

RICHARD SOLOMON ▪ ARTIST REPRESENTATIVE ▪ 121 MADISON AVE. ▪ NYC 10016 ▪ (212) 683-1362 ▪ FAX: (212) 683-1919

ROBERT PLANT / MIXED MEDIA

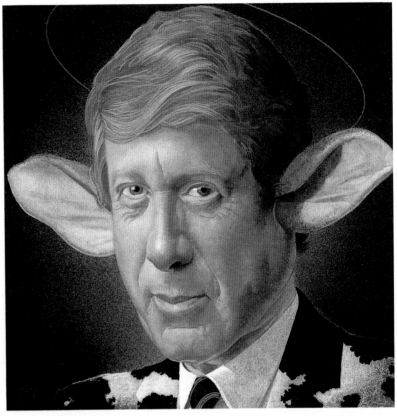

WASHINGTON SACRED COW, TED KOPPEL

PETER HASS, PRESIDENT & CEO, LEVI STRAUSS

FOUR EYES & TWENTY FINGERS

RICHARD SOLOMON • ARTIST REPRESENTATIVE • 121 MADISON AVE. • NYC 10016 • (212) 683-1362 • FAX: (212) 683-1919

JESSE JACKSON ADDRESSES 1988 DEMOCRATIC NATIONAL CONVENTION / PEN & INK

BILL BUCKLEY SEEKS A CURE

NORMAN MAILER "LIT" INTO GORE VIDAL

RICHARD SOLOMON • ARTIST REPRESENTATIVE • 121 MADISON AVE. • NYC 10016 • (212) 683-1362 • FAX: (212) 683-1919

NEW YORK: HELL'S KITCHEN, 1930 / PENCIL

RICHARD SOLOMON • ARTIST REPRESENTATIVE • 121 MADISON AVE. • NYC 10016 • (212) 683-1362 • FAX: (212) 683-1919

FORTUNES MAY DEPEND ON THE WINE MASTERS' VERDICT — INTERNATIONAL WINE CENTER

POMEROL IS AN EXCITING RED WINE, WELL ROUNDED, FLESHY AND QUICK-MATURING — INTERNATIONAL WINE CENTER

ANIMATION & ANIMATICS REEL AVAILABLE

CHARLES GEHM

REPRESENTED BY JERRY LEFF ASSOCIATES, INC. ■ 420 LEXINGTON AVE. NEW YORK CITY 10170 ■ TEL: (212) 697-8525 ■ FAX: (212) 949-1843

HOT MONEY BY DICK FRANCIS

Available for portrait commissions.

FRANCO ACCORNERO

REPRESENTED BY JERRY LEFF ASSOCIATES, INC. ■ 420 LEXINGTON AVE. NEW YORK CITY 10170 ■ TEL: (212) 697-8525 ■ FAX: (212) 949-1843

Available for portrait commissions.

TERRY HOFF

REPRESENTED BY JERRY LEFF ASSOCIATES, INC. ■ 420 LEXINGTON AVE. NEW YORK CITY 10170 ■ TEL: (212) 697-8525 ■ FAX: (212) 949-1843

SAN FRANCISCO
FREDA SCOTT

TEL: (415) 621-2992
FAX: (415) 621-5202

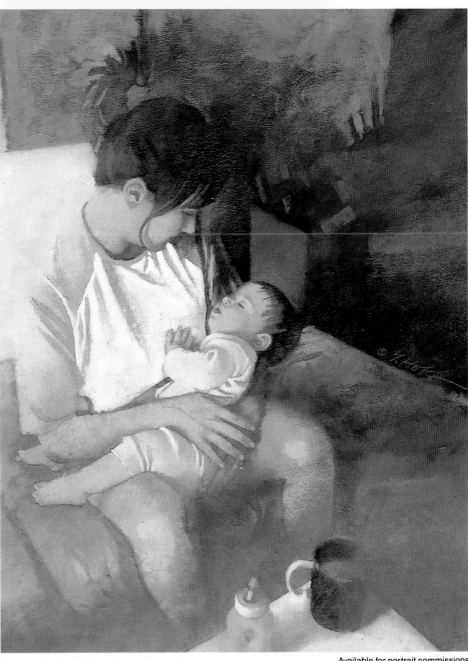

Available for portrait commissions.

JUDY YORK

REPRESENTED BY JERRY LEFF ASSOCIATES, INC. ■ *420 LEXINGTON AVE. NEW YORK CITY 10170* ■ *TEL: (212) 697-8525* ■ *FAX: (212) 949-1843*

Available for portrait commissions.

RON DICIANNI

REPRESENTED BY JERRY LEFF ASSOCIATES, INC. ■ 420 LEXINGTON AVE. NEW YORK CITY 10170 ■ TEL: (212) 697-8525 ■ FAX: (212) 949-1843

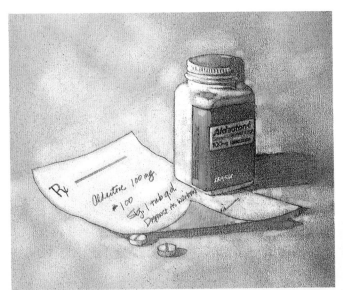

Available for portrait commissions

CELIA MITCHELL

REPRESENTED BY JERRY LEFF ASSOCIATES, INC. ■ 420 LEXINGTON AVE. NEW YORK CITY 10170 ■ TEL: (212) 697-8525 ■ FAX: (212) 949-1843

Available for portrait commissions.

RON LESSER

REPRESENTED BY JERRY LEFF ASSOCIATES, INC. ■ 420 LEXINGTON AVE. NEW YORK CITY 10170 ■ TEL: (212) 697-8525 ■ FAX: (212) 949-1843

Available for portrait commissions.

Available for portrait commissions.

ALEX BOIES

REPRESENTED BY JERRY LEFF ASSOCIATES, INC. ■ 420 LEXINGTON AVE. NEW YORK CITY 10170 ■ TEL: (212) 697-8525 ■ FAX: (212) 949-1843

ALAN MAZZETTI

REPRESENTED BY JERRY LEFF ASSOCIATES, INC. ■ 420 LEXINGTON AVE. NEW YORK CITY 10170 ■ TEL: (212) 697-8525 ■ FAX: (212) 949-1843

SAN FRANCISCO
FREDA SCOTT

TEL: (415) 621-2992
FAX: (415) 621-5202

GARY McLAUGHLIN

REPRESENTED BY JERRY LEFF ASSOCIATES, INC. ■ 420 LEXINGTON AVE. NEW YORK CITY 10170 ■ TEL: (212) 697-8525 ■ FAX: (212) 949-1843

Available for portrait commissions.

REPRESENTED BY JERRY LEFF ASSOCIATES, INC. ■ 420 LEXINGTON AVE. NEW YORK CITY 10170 ■ TEL: (212) 697-8525 ■ FAX: (212) 949-1843

DENNIS MAGDICH

REPRESENTED BY JERRY LEFF ASSOCIATES, INC. ■ 420 LEXINGTON AVE. NEW YORK CITY 10170 ■ TEL: (212) 697-8525 ■ FAX: (212) 949-1843
IN THE SOUTHWEST CALL JUDY ■ TEL: (505) 984-8534 ■ FAX: (505) 984-8734

KENN RICHARDS

PENELOPE

REPRESENTED BY JERRY LEFF ASSOCIATES, INC. ■ 420 LEXINGTON AVE. NEW YORK CITY 10170 ■ TEL: (212) 697-8525 ■ FAX: (212) 949-1843

50% More Free!! BONUS PACK

THE
BREAK
WITH
TRADITION

SAUCE RECIPE BOOK
FROM OPEN PIT* BARBECUE SAUCE

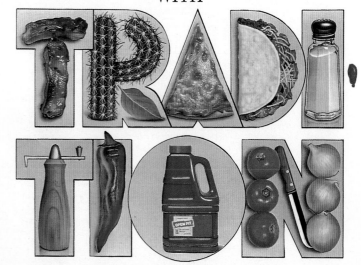

SEMYON BILMES

SEMYON BILMES

VICKI MORGAN ASSOC.

194 THIRD AVENUE NEW YORK NY 10003

(212) 475·0440

WARD SCHUMAKER

SONOMA CITY HALL   SCHUMAKER

NANCY STAHL

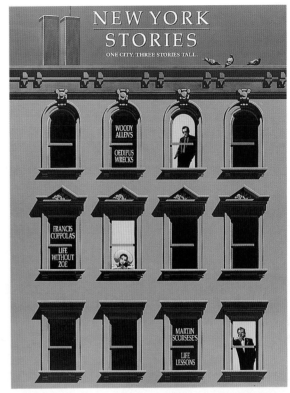

194 THIRD AVENUE NEW YORK NY 10003
VICKI MORGAN ASSOC.
(212) 475·0440

183

PATTY DRYDEN

VICKI MORGAN ASSOC.
194 THIRD AVENUE NEW YORK NY 10003
(212) 475·0440

VIVIENNE FLESHER

194 THIRD AVENUE NEW YORK NY 10003
VICKI MORGAN ASSOC.
(212) 475·0440

JOANIE SCHWARZ

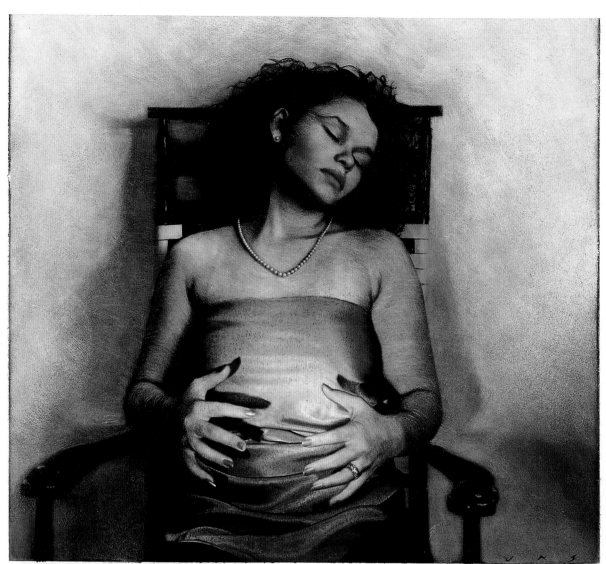

194 THIRD AVENUE NEW YORK NY 10003
VICKI MORGAN ASSOC.
(212) 475·0440

JOYCE PATTI

NANETTE BIERS

194 THIRD AVENUE NEW YORK NY 10003
VICKI MORGAN ASSOC.
(212) 475·0440

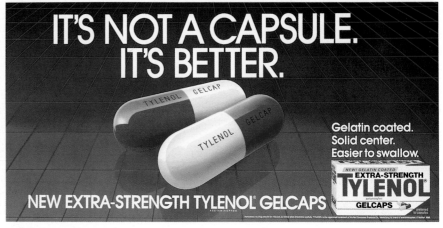

IT'S NOT A CAPSULE.
IT'S BETTER.

Gelatin coated.
Solid center.
Easier to swallow.

NEW EXTRA-STRENGTH TYLENOL GELCAPS

RAY CRUZ

BRIAN ZICK

"X" MARKS THE SPOT

WUF

PICK YOUR FAVORITES   PICK YOUR PLEASURE   PICK THE BEST   PICK-A-MIX

VICKI MORGAN ASSOC.
194 THIRD AVENUE NEW YORK NY 10003
(212) 475-0440

WENDY WRAY

194 THIRD AVENUE NEW YORK NY 10003

VICKI **M**ORGAN **A**SSOC.

(212) 475·0440

DAHL TAYLOR

LAVATY

Gervasio Gallardo
Chris Duke
John Berkey
Don Daily
Stan Hunter
Jim Butcher
Carlos Ochagavia
Mort Kunstler
Lemuel Line
Martin Hoffman
David McCall Johnston
Roland DesCombes
Tim Hildebrandt
Robert Lo Grippo
Bruce Emmett
Bernard D'Andrea
Paul Lehr
Ben Verkaaik

Represented by
Frank Lavaty
Jeff Lavaty
Steven Kenny

Frank & Jeff Lavaty & Associates • 509 Madison Avenue N.Y. N.Y. 10022 • (212) 355-0910

Frank and Jeff Lavaty
& Associates
509 Madison Avenue
New York, New York 10022
(212) 355-0910 Fax in office

Representing:
Gervasio Gallardo

LAVATY

**Frank and Jeff Lavaty
& Associates**

509 Madison Avenue
New York, New York 10022
(212) 355-0910 Fax in office

Representing:
Chris Duke

LAVATY

Frank and Jeff Lavaty
& Associates

509 Madison Avenue
New York, New York 10022
(212) 355-0910 Fax in office

Representing:
John Berkey

LAVATY

**Frank and Jeff Lavaty
& Associates**

509 Madison Avenue
New York, New York 10022
(212) 355-0910 Fax in office

Representing:
Don Daily

LAVATY

**Frank and Jeff Lavaty
& Associates**

509 Madison Avenue
New York, New York 10022
(212) 355-0910 Fax in office

Representing:
Stan Hunter

LAVATY

Frank and Jeff Lavaty
& Associates

509 Madison Avenue
New York, New York 10022
(212) 355-0910 Fax in office

Representing:
Jim Butcher

LAVATY

Frank and Jeff Lavaty
& Associates

509 Madison Avenue
New York, New York 10022
(212) 355-0910 Fax in office

Representing:
Carlos Ochagavia

**Frank and Jeff Lavaty
& Associates**

509 Madison Avenue
New York, New York 10022
(212) 355-0910 Fax in office

Representing:
Mort Kunstler

Frank and Jeff Lavaty
& Associates

509 Madison Avenue
New York, New York 10022
(212) 355-0910 Fax in office

Representing:
Lemuel Line

LAVATY

**Frank and Jeff Lavaty
& Associates**

509 Madison Avenue
New York, New York 10022
(212) 355-0910 Fax in office

Representing:
Martin Hoffman

LAVATY

**Frank and Jeff Lavaty
& Associates**

509 Madison Avenue
New York, New York 10022
(212) 355-0910 Fax in office

Representing:
David McCall Johnston

LAVATY

**Frank and Jeff Lavaty
& Associates**

509 Madison Avenue
New York, New York 10022
(212) 355-0910 Fax in office

Representing:
Roland DesCombes

LAVATY

R. DesCombes

**Frank and Jeff Lavaty
& Associates**

509 Madison Avenue
New York, New York 10022
(212) 355-0910 Fax in office

Representing:
Tim Hildebrandt

LAVATY

**Frank and Jeff Lavaty
& Associates**

509 Madison Avenue
New York, New York 10022
(212) 355-0910 Fax in office

Representing:
Robert Lo Grippo

LAVATY

**Frank and Jeff Lavaty
& Associates**

509 Madison Avenue
New York, New York 10022
(212) 355-0910 Fax in office

Representing:
Bruce Emmett

LAVATY

DOUG SUMA

Represented by:
Daniele Collignon

200 West 15th Street
New York, NY 10011

Phone (212) 243-4209
Fax (212) 463-0634

DANIELE
COLLIGNON

BILL FRAMPTON

Represented by:
Daniele Collignon

200 West 15th Street
New York, NY 10011

Phone (212) 243-4209
Fax (212) 463-0634

1

2

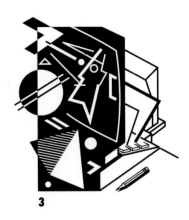

3

4

5

6

7

8

9

10

11

1. Cranwell Pietrasiak Design 2. Kelloggs Nutrition Conference 3. Comac 4. Sentinel Heating
5. Provincial Graphics 6. Who's Who 7. The Riordon Group 8. U.S.Sprint 9. Tom Benedict 10. High Voltage
12. Provincial Graphics

DAN COSGROVE

Represented by:
Daniele Collignon

200 West 15th Street
New York, NY 10011

Phone (212) 243-4209
Fax (212) 463-0634

IRENA ROMAN

Represented by:
Daniele Collignon

200 West 15th Street
New York, NY 10011

Phone (212) 243-4209
Fax (212) 463-0634

DANIELE
COLLIGNON

HISASHI SEKINE

Represented by:
Daniele Collignon

200 West 15th Street
New York, NY 10011

Phone (212) 243-4209
Fax (212) 463-0634

DANIELE COLLIGNON

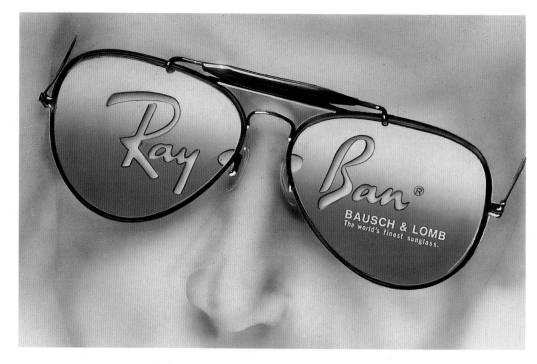

STEVE LYONS

Represented by:
Daniele Collignon

200 West 15th Street
New York, NY 10011

Phone (212) 243-4209
Fax (212) 463-0634

MITCH O'CONNELL

Represented by:
Daniele Collignon

200 West 15th Street
New York, NY 10011

Phone (212) 243-4209
Fax (212) 463-0634

DON WELLER

Represented by:
Daniele Collignon

200 West 15th Street
New York, NY 10011

Phone (212) 243-4209
Fax (212) 463-0634

CINDY PARDY

Represented by:
Daniele Collignon

200 West 15th Street
New York, NY 10011

Phone (212) 243-4209
Fax (212) 463-0634

DANIELE
COLLIGNON

He's recording on **AGFA**

AUDIO VIDEO PROFESSIONAL

She's listening to **AGFA**

AUDIO VIDEO PROFESSIONAL

Hand Tinting on Photographs, Yours or Mine

ALEX TIANI

Represented by:
Daniele Collignon

200 West 15th Street
New York, NY 10011

Phone (212) 243-4209
Fax (212) 463-0634

David Lesh

Representative:
Joanne Palulian
18 McKinley Street
Rowayton, CT 06853

(203) 866-3734
(212) 581-8338

David Lesh

David Lesh

Representative:
Joanne Palulian
18 McKinley Street
Rowayton, CT 06853

(203) 866-3734
(212) 581-8338

Bonnie Hofkin
Medical Illustration

Representative:
Joanne Palulian
18 McKinley Street
Rowayton, CT 06853

(203) 866-3734
(212) 581-8338

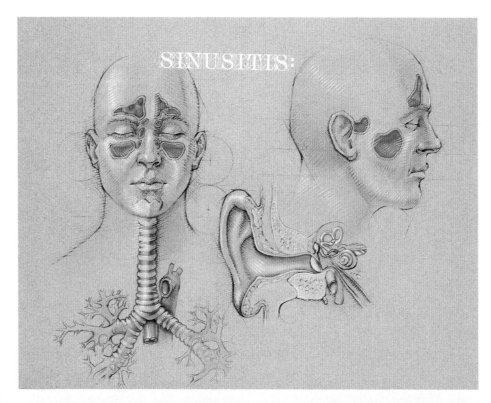

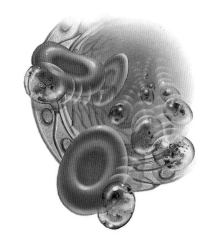

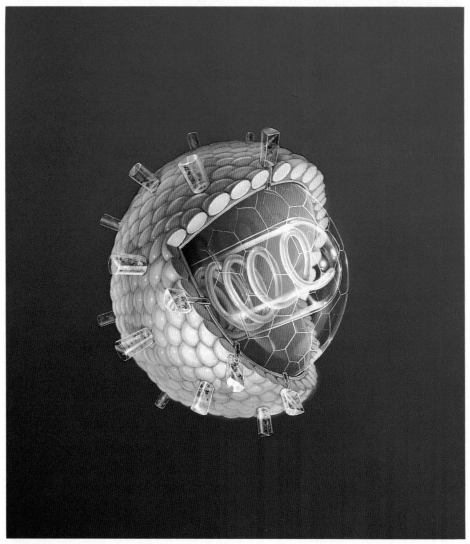

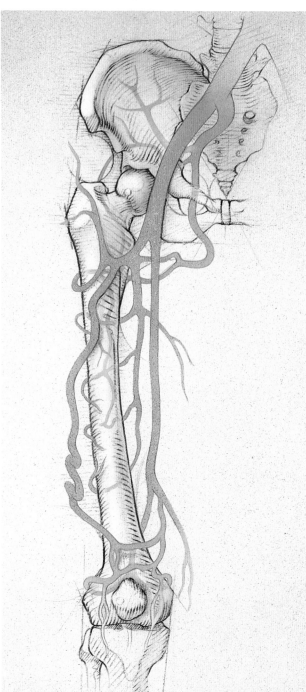

When you need quality illustration and you can't afford to fool around...consult

THE ULTIMATE AUTHORITY

You have enough problems as it is. So give yourself a break.

Spare yourself that familiar sinking feeling when the deadline day comes and the illustration you ordered still isn't quite right or quite ready.

When you need quality illustration and you can't afford to fool around, why not consult The Ultimate Authority? Call Gerald & Cullen Rapp, Inc.

There's got to be a reason why we probably sell more quality illustration than anyone else. And there is.

We not only represent an impressive group of the nation's most talented illustrators and cartoonists.

We offer superb service, based on 41 years of experience, to help you meet expectations and deadlines with minimum fuss and hassle.

When you buy from an unknown illustrator, based on two or three reproduced samples, you really have no way of knowing what you are getting into.

Were those pieces really typical? How long did they take? How many revisions were needed? How much guidance did they require from an A.D.?

But we have been dealing with each of our recognized artists for an average of 15 years. We know exactly what we can expect and what you can expect.

We can give you lightning two-way communication. Call us about your needs. We'll fax you quotes and pencil sketches.

And if we can't help you, we'll suggest who might be able to.

So the next time you need the right illustration at the right time, don't be overwhelmed by the hundreds of possibilities.

Give yourself a break.

Give us a ring.

Meanwhile see the outer back cover for our file box offer.

Gerald & Cullen Rapp, Inc.
108 East 35 St. (#1), New York, NY 10016 • (212) 889-3337 • Fax (212) 889-3341

GERALD & CULLEN RAPP, INC.
108 East 35 St. (#1), New York 10016
(212) 889-3337 • Fax (212) 889-3341

EMMANUEL
AMIT

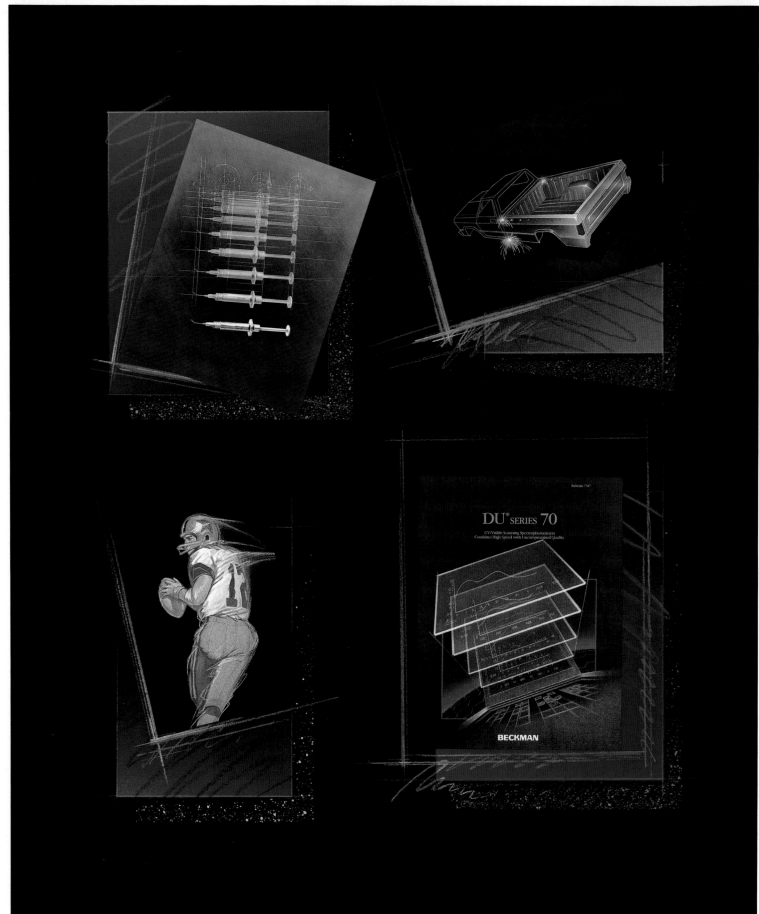

GERALD & CULLEN RAPP, INC.
108 East 35 St. (# 1), New York 10016
(212) 889-3337 • Fax (212) 889-3341

MICHAEL DAVID BROWN

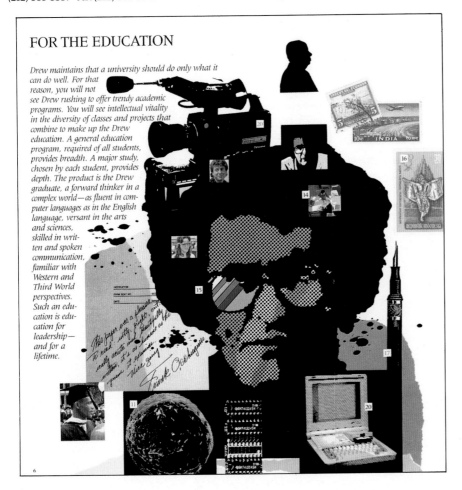

FOR THE EDUCATION

Drew maintains that a university should do only what it can do well. For that reason, you will not see Drew rushing to offer trendy academic programs. You will see intellectual vitality in the diversity of classes and projects that combine to make up the Drew education. A general education program, required of all students, provides breadth. A major study, chosen by each student, provides depth. The product is the Drew graduate, a forward thinker in a complex world—as fluent in computer languages as in the English language, versant in the arts and sciences, skilled in written and spoken communication, familiar with Western and Third World perspectives. Such an education is education for leadership—and for a lifetime.

Kent.
The choice is taste.

KENT   KENT Golden Lights   KENT III

The low-tar family with taste.

SURGEON GENERAL'S WARNING: Cigarette Smoke Contains Carbon Monoxide.

1989 CALENDAR
Franklin Square Hospital Center

227

LON
BUSCH

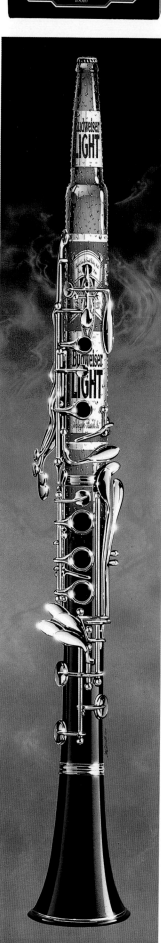

GERALD & CULLEN RAPP, INC.
108 East 35 St. (#1), New York 10016
(212) 889-3337 • Fax (212) 889-3341

JACK DAVIS

When allergy symptoms have customers searching for relief...

NEW YORK, N.Y.

BOB
DESCHAMPS

BILL
DEVLIN

LEE DUGGAN

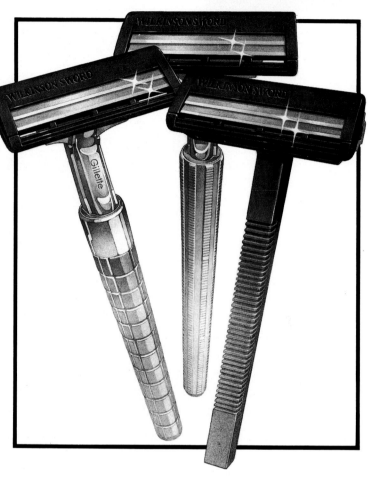

L E E
DUGGAN

The Berry Bears® were happily gathering the delicious fruit snacks that look just like them. "I've filled 3 baskets!" said Belinda. "You're fillin' and I'm-*whummmp-spillin'!*" exclaimed Bobby, as he tripped over a Berry Bear basket. "Whoa, Belinda!" yelled Papa. "Pick the Berry Bear berries, not my tail!" "Speaking of tails... where's the tail of my littlest Baby Bear?" wondered Mama. "Hee hee!" The Berry Bears heard Baby Bear giggling, but couldn't find him any*where*! Can you find Baby Bear hiding in the picture? Or, meet him and his fantastically fruity family in every fun box of The Berry Bears!

FRUIT CORNER®
MADE WITH REAL FRUIT
The BERRY BEARS
CHEWY FRUIT SNACKS
NEW
6 POUCHES **ASSORTED FRUIT** NET WT. 5.4 OZ
Fantastically Fruity!

233

R A N D Y
GLASS

SURPRISE! FREE FRIES

LIONEL
KALISH

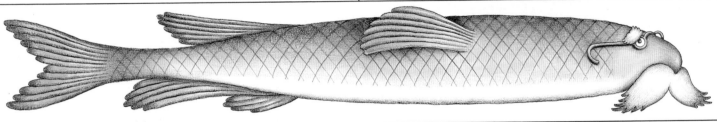

L A S Z L O
KUBINYI

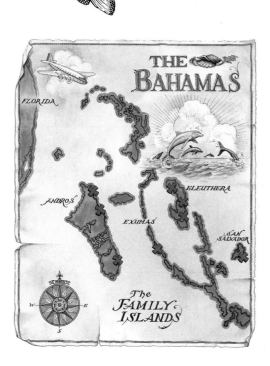

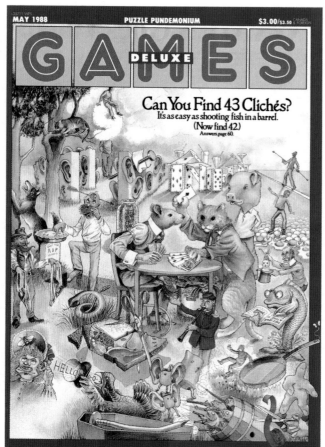

L E E
LORENZ

LESS CHOLESTOROL
REGULAR CHECKUPS
NO NICOTINE
NO ALCOHOL
LOW SODIUM
MODERATE EXERCISE
NO SUGAR

GERALD & CULLEN RAPP, INC.
108 East 35 St. (#1), New York 10016
(212) 889-3337 • Fax (212) 889-3341

ALLAN MARDON

238

GERALD & CULLEN RAPP, INC.
108 East 35 St. (#1), New York 10016
(212) 889-3337 • Fax (212) 889-3341

A L E X
MURAWSKI

LOU
MYERS

LA CAGE FOLLES

SALES

COSTS

BARNES & NOBLE

SALE/ANNEX

GERALD & CULLEN RAPP, INC.
108 East 35 St. (#1), New York 10016
(212) 889-3337 • Fax (212) 889-3341

BOB PETERS

GERALD & CULLEN RAPP, INC.
108 East 35 St. (#1), New York 10016
(212) 889-3337 • Fax (212) 889-3341

CAMILLE PRZEWODEK

GERALD & CULLEN RAPP, INC.
108 East 35 St. (# 1), New York 10016
(212) 889-3337 • Fax (212) 889-3341

ROBERT
TANENBAUM

MICHAEL WITTE

ICE COLD CHARGERS

IT'S JUST NOT FAIR, YOU ALWAYS HAVE BETTER MIRAGES THAN I DO!

Charger: Sparkling water, two dashes of Angostura and a wedge of lime.

ANGOSTURA AROMATIC BITTERS

245

IRMELI HOLMBERG

IRMELI HOLMBERG / ARTIST AGENT / 280 MADISON AVENUE / ROOM 1402 / NEW YORK / NY 10016 / TEL: 212-545-9155
FAX: 212-545-9462

TWELFTH NIGHT

CAT ON A HOT TIN ROOF

ALL GOD'S DANGERS

MACBETH

SHAKESPEARE FESTIVAL

Cyd Moore

C Y D M O O R E

246

IRMELI HOLMBERG

IRMELI HOLMBERG / ARTIST AGENT / 280 MADISON AVENUE / ROOM 1402 / NEW YORK / NY 10016 / TEL: 212-545-9155
FAX: 212-545-9462

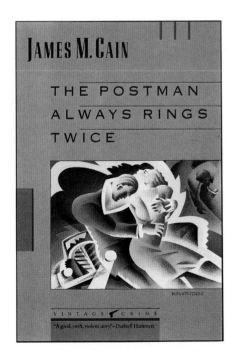

NIKOLAI PUNIN

IRMELI HOLMBERG / ARTIST AGENT / 280 MADISON AVENUE / ROOM 1402 / NEW YORK / NY 10016 / TEL: 212-545-9155
FAX: 212-545-9462

DEBORAH PINKNEY

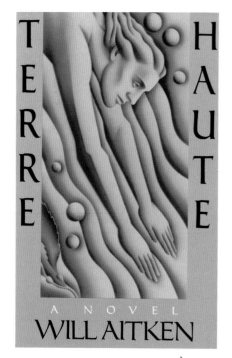

MARILYN MONTGOMERY

IRMELI HOLMBERG

IRMELI HOLMBERG / ARTIST AGENT / 280 MADISON AVENUE / ROOM 1402 / NEW YORK / NY 10016 / TEL: 212-545-9155
FAX: 212-545-9462

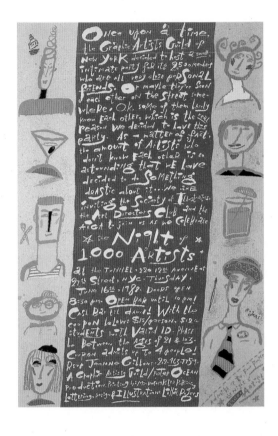

L I L L A   R O G E R S

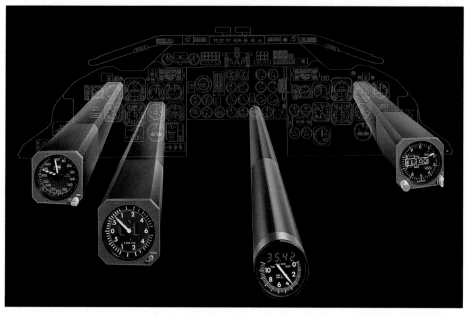

L U   M A T T H E W S

IRMELI HOLMBERG

IRMELI HOLMBERG / ARTIST AGENT / 280 MADISON AVENUE / ROOM 1402 / NEW YORK / NY 10016 / TEL: 212-545-9155
FAX: 212-545-9462

RANDIE WASSERMAN

IRMELI HOLMBERG

IRMELI HOLMBERG / ARTIST AGENT / 280 MADISON AVENUE / ROOM 1402 / NEW YORK / NY 10016 / TEL: 212-545-9155
FAX: 212-545-9462

ANDREW PAQUETTE

DAN BRIDY

TEL: 412/288/9362

IRMELI HOLMBERG

IRMELI HOLMBERG / ARTIST AGENT / 280 MADISON AVENUE / ROOM 1402 / NEW YORK / NY 10016 / TEL: 212-545-9155
FAX: 212-545-9462

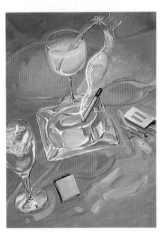

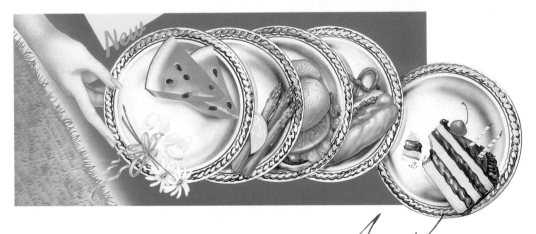

A N N   N E U M A N N

IRMELI HOLMBERG

IRMELI HOLMBERG / ARTIST AGENT / 280 MADISON AVENUE / ROOM 1402 / NEW YORK / NY 10016 / TEL: 212-545-9155
FAX: 212-545-9462

Athletes & Entertainers for Kids present Kareem: celebrating the career of a legend, 1989 Benefit Dinner Gala
Monday evening, April 24th, 1989, Century Plaza Hotel, Avenue of the Stars, Century City, California, Black Tie

TEL: 213/318/1837

WILLIAM RIESER

IRMELI HOLMBERG

IRMELI HOLMBERG / ARTIST AGENT / 280 MADISON AVENUE / ROOM 1402 / NEW YORK / NY 10016 / TEL: 212-545-9155
FAX: 212-545-9462

T O Y C E   A N D E R S O N

Charles Krug

Chenin Blanc

Cabernet Sauvignon

Sauvignon Blanc

First in Napa Valley

ESTABLISHED 1861

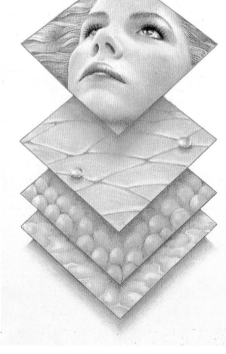

JACQUELINE OSBORN

in San Francisco contact Kathy Braun: 415/775/3366

IRMELI HOLMBERG

IRMELI HOLMBERG / ARTIST AGENT / 280 MADISON AVENUE / ROOM 1402 / NEW YORK / NY 10016 / TEL: 212-545-9155
FAX: 212-545-9462

DIE TOTE STADT

STREET SCENE

IL BARBIERE DI SIVIGLIA

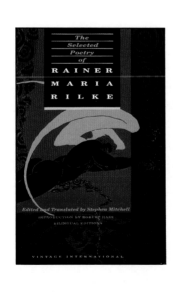

J O H N   M A R T I N E Z

What's next?

It isn't surprising that our critics don't see eye to eye with us about <u>Channel One</u> news.

ROBERT BERGIN

INCANDESCENT INK, INC. 111 WOOSTER STREET PHC. NEW YORK, N.Y. 10012

REPRESENTED BY LES MINTZ (212) 925-0491

Please contact us to receive our new color brochures if you have not yet gotten them. Thank you

BERNARD BONHOMME

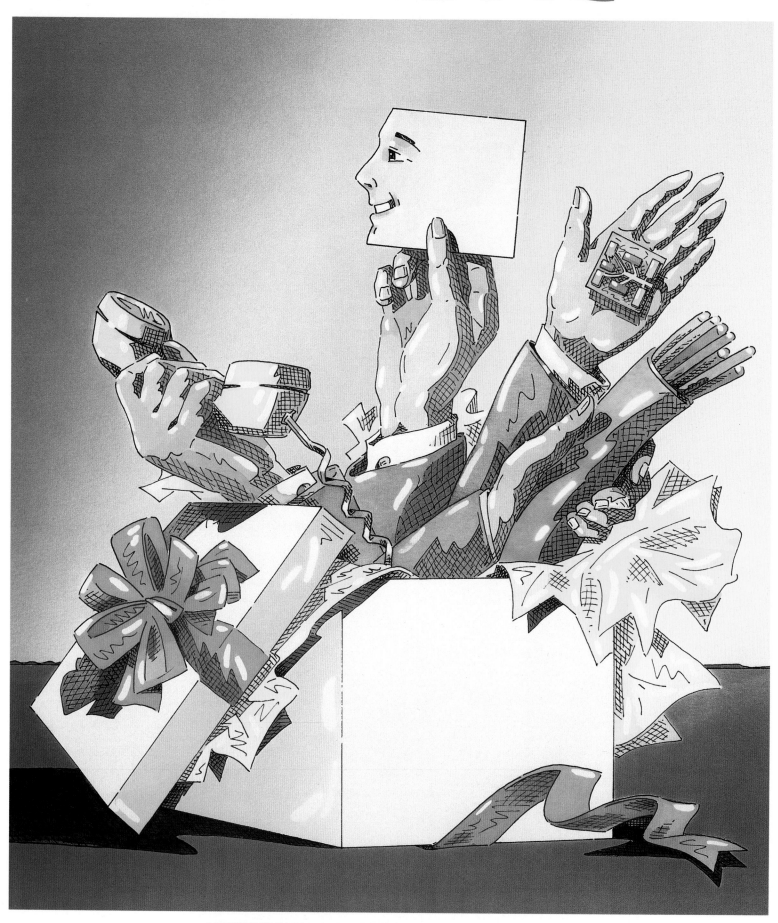

MARK FISHER

INCANDESCENT INK, INC. 111 WOOSTER STREET PHC. NEW YORK, N.Y. 10012
REPRESENTED BY LES MINTZ (212) 925-0491

Please contact us to receive our new color brochures if you have not yet gotten them. Thank you

MARK FRESH

INCANDESCENT INK, INC. 111 WOOSTER STREET PHC. NEW YORK, N.Y. 10012

REPRESENTED BY LES MINTZ (212) 925-0491

Please contact us to receive our new color brochures if you have not yet gotten them. Thank you

ROBERTA LUDLOW

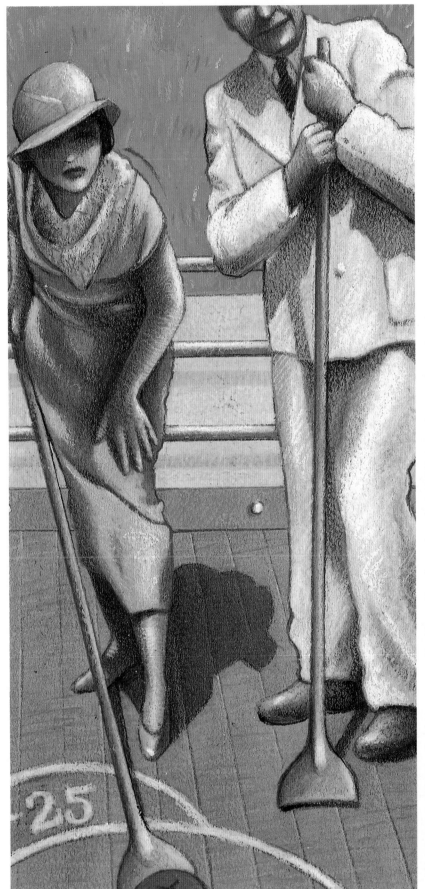

INCANDESCENT INK, INC. 111 WOOSTER STREET PHC. NEW YORK, N.Y. 10012

REPRESENTED BY LES MINTZ (212) 925-0491

Please contact us to receive our new color brochures if you have not yet gotten them. Thank you

DAVID LUI

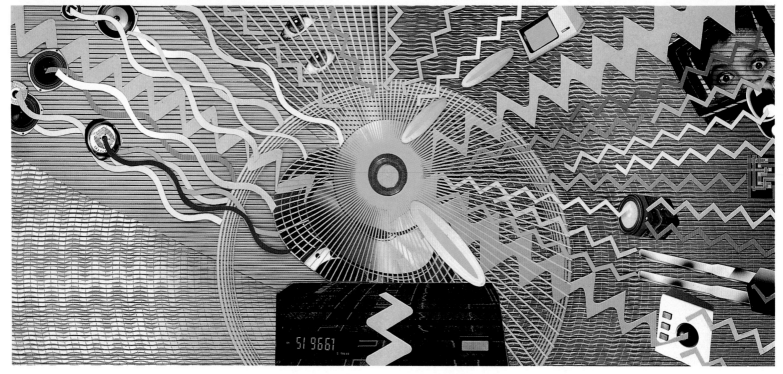

INCANDESCENT INK, INC. 111 WOOSTER STREET PHC. NEW YORK, N.Y. 10012
REPRESENTED BY LES MINTZ (212) 925-0491

Please contact us to receive our new color brochures if you have not yet gotten them. Thank you

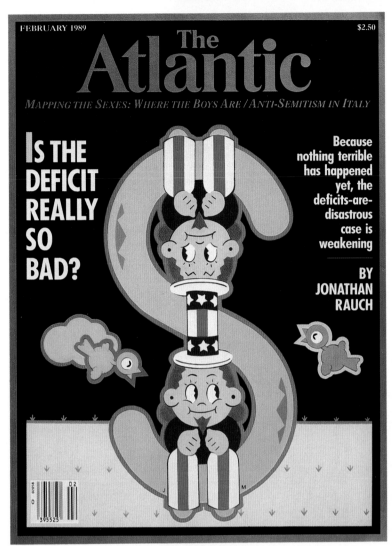

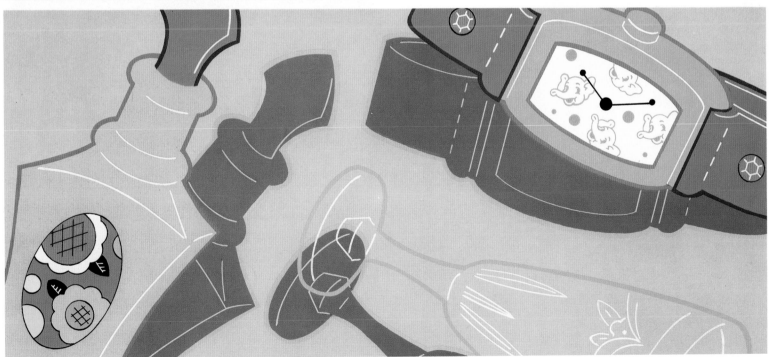

JUDITH SUTTON

INCANDESCENT INK, INC. 111 WOOSTER STREET PHC. NEW YORK, N.Y. 10012

REPRESENTED BY LES MINTZ (212) 925-0491

Please contact us to receive our new color brochures if you have not yet gotten them. Thank you

SARAH WALDRON

3525 Mockingbird Lane
Dallas, Texas 75205.2225
214.521.5156
Fax 214.520.6366

Lee Lee Brazeal

3525 Mockingbird Lane
Dallas, Texas 75205.2225
214.521.5156
Fax 214.520.6366

ART
REP
INC

Greg King

3525 Mockingbird Lane
Dallas, Texas 75205.2225
214.521.5156
Fax 214.520.6366

In New York City, Joanne Palulian,
212.581.8338

ART
REP
INC

M. John English

3525 Mockingbird Lane
Dallas, Texas 75205.2225
214.521.5156
Fax 214.520.6366

ART
REP
INC

Stephen Turk

TAKE A CLOSER LOOK AT AT&T INTERNATIONAL SERVICES.

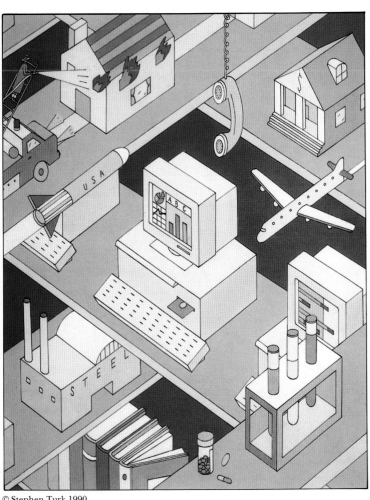

3525 Mockingbird Lane
Dallas, Texas 75205.2225
214.521.5156
Fax 214.520.6366

ART REP INC Lindy Chambers

3525 Mockingbird Lane
Dallas, Texas 75205.2225
214.521.5156
Fax 214.520.6366

In New York City, Ron Puhalski, Inc.
212.242.2860

Ellis Chappell

3525 Mockingbird Lane
Dallas, Texas 75205.2225
214.521.5156
Fax 214.520.6366

ART REP INC

Tom Dolphens

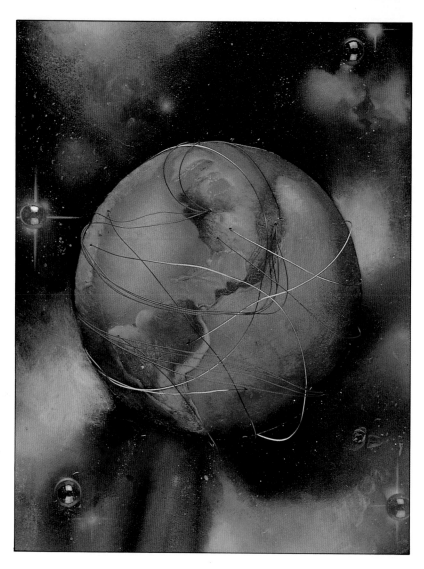

3525 Mockingbird Lane
Dallas, Texas 75205.2225
214.521.5156
Fax 214.520.6366

ART
REP
INC

Jim Jacobs

*Your
one-stop shop
for cats*

———

*With experience
as well in
household appliances
women playing accordions
bicycles*

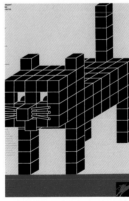

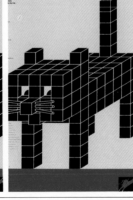

*likable software,
canned goods,
houses with arms and legs,
video recorders,
cows,
earnest businessmen,
hip kids,
BMW mechanics and
trout.*

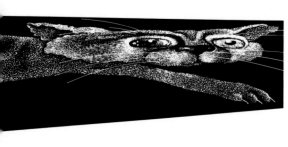

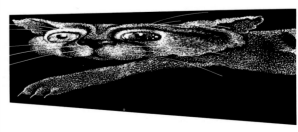

© Jim Jacobs 1990

277

RILEY ILLUSTRATION

J.J. Sempé

Pierre Le-Tan

Robert Andrew Parker

Paul Meisel

David Small

William Bramhall

Chris Demarest

Representing: William Bramhall,   Paul Degen,   Chris Demarest,   Pierre Le-Tan,   Paul Meisel,   Robert Andrew Parker,
Jim Parkinson Lettering,   J.J. Sempé,   David Small   & Other Artists

Whit Stillman, Director   (212) 925-3053   RILEY ILLUSTRATION   81 Greene St. New York, NY 10012

212·473·8747

SUSAN **G**OMBERG

**ARTISTS
REPRESENTATIVE**

James Tughan

Robert Dale

Jeff Leedy

Allen Garns

Ralph Giguere

Jacobson/Fernandez

Mark Weakley

Neil Brennan

Sheckman/Ferguson

Dan McGowan

Enzo Messi & Urs Schmidt

212·473·8747

SUSAN GOMBERG

ARTISTS
REPRESENTATIVE

Fax: (212) 473-9521

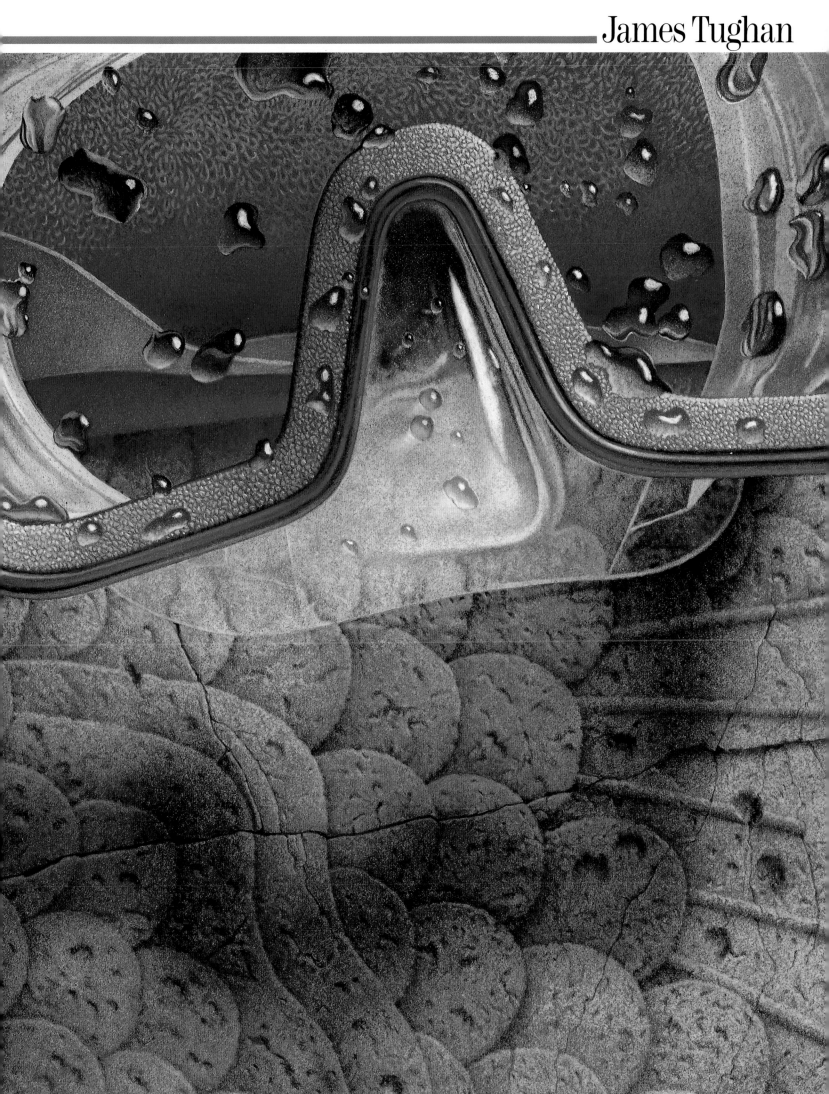

Jeff Leedy

Fax: (212) 473-9521

212·473·8747

SUSAN **G**OMBERG

ARTISTS
REPRESENTATIVE

In San Francisco: Nona Amour (415) 459 0319
In Los Angeles: Rena Natale (213) 399-4891

212·473·8747

Fax: (212) 473-9521

SUSAN **G**OMBERG

ARTISTS
REPRESENTATIVE

Ralph Giguere

Fax: (212) 473-9521
In Philadelphia: Robert Rotella (215) 968-3696/Fax: (215) 968-8828

212·473·8747

SUSAN **G**OMBERG

ARTISTS
REPRESENTATIVE

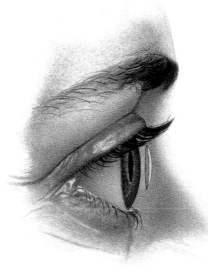

The tire that tamed the wild west.
And still the best.

LAREDO

Fax: (212) 473-9521

212·473·8747

SUSAN GOMBERG

ARTISTS
REPRESENTATIVE

212·473·8747

Fax: (212) 473-9521

SUSAN **G**OMBERG

ARTISTS REPRESENTATIVE

Mark Weakley

Neil Brennan

Fax: (212) 473-9521

212·473·8747

SUSAN **G**OMBERG

ARTISTS
REPRESENTATIVE

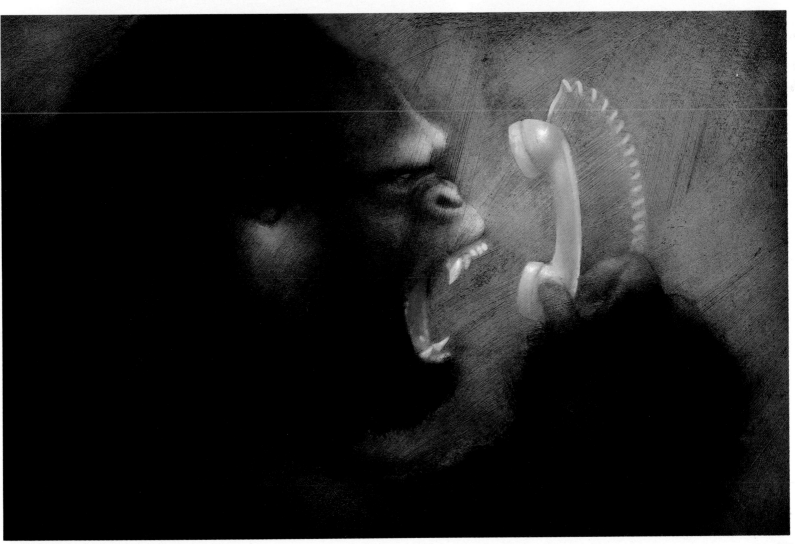

212·473·8747   Fax: (212) 473-9521

SUSAN **GOMBERG**
ARTISTS REPRESENTATIVE

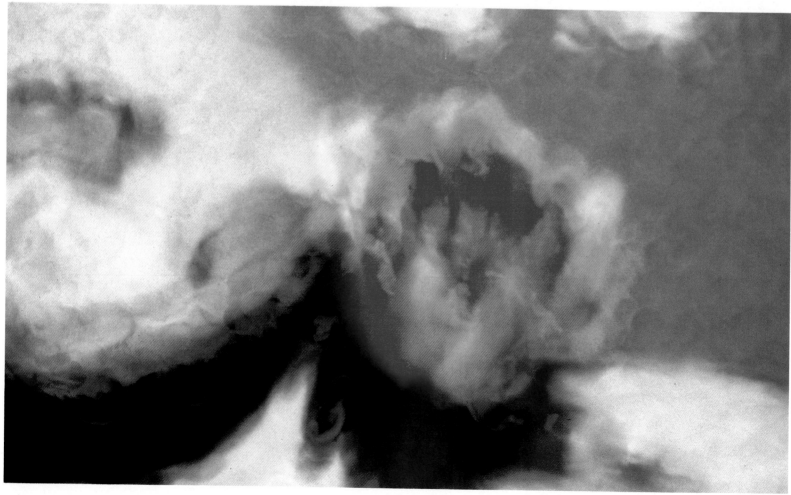

Dan McGowan

Fax: (212) 473-9521

212·473·8747

SUSAN **G**OMBERG

ARTISTS
REPRESENTATIVE

Fax: (212) 473-9521

212·473·8747

SUSAN **G**OMBERG

ARTISTS
REPRESENTATIVE

JOHN BURGOYNE

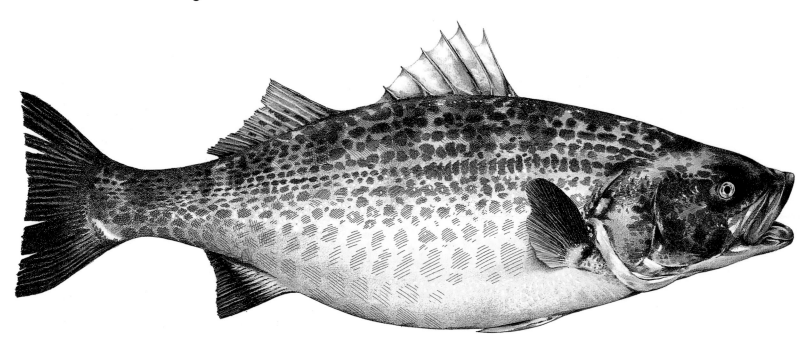

ILLUSTRATORS
Katherine
TISE
212·570·9069
200 East 78th Street
New York. N.Y. 10021
REPRESENTATIVE

JOHN BURGOYNE

RAPHAEL BOGUSLAV

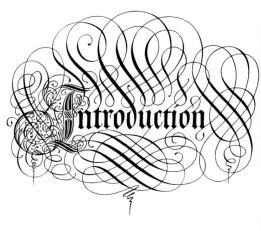

The Providence Journal Company Album

Cranberry Sauce

BROWN & HOWARD
NEWPORT. RHODE ISLAND

Introduction

THE NEWPORT Gilded Age COLLECTION

WESTWARD

EAST RIVER 21 STREET

SunStreaks

Ryan's

Dodge

Rothenburg

PP

NEW YORK LIFE

Holiday gift

A

New HAMPSHIRE

Cafe LA PATISSERIE

PANORAMA · SPECIAL REPORT
1981
THE YEAR IN REVIEW

1981
Jonathan Logan Inc.
Annual Report

PPG

Raphael Boguslav 52 Thames Street Newport, RI 02840 fax avaliable

Logotypes, lettering of all kinds, calligraphy, package design, ornament, etc. etc.

Represented by Katherine Tise 212 570 9069

NEAL HUGHES

REPRESENTED BY: **DEBORAH WOLFE LTD**
731 N. 24th ST., PHILA., PA 19130
215 / 232-6666
FAX 215 / 232-6585

ERIC JOYNER

REPRESENTED BY: **DEBORAH WOLFE LTD**
731 N. 24th ST., PHILA., PA 19130
215 / 232-6666
FAX 215 / 232-6585
IN SF 415/459-1448

SKIP BAKER

REPRESENTED BY: **DEBORAH WOLFE LTD**
731 N. 24th ST., PHILA., PA 19130
215 / 232-6666
FAX 215 / 232-6585

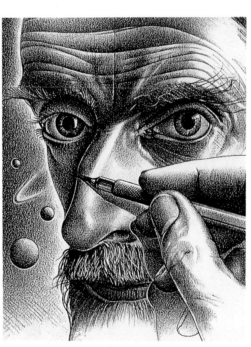

299

NICK GAETANO

HARVEY KAHN

212 752-8490

14 EAST 52 STREET, NEW YORK, NY 10022

FAX: 212-753-1721

ROBERT PEAK

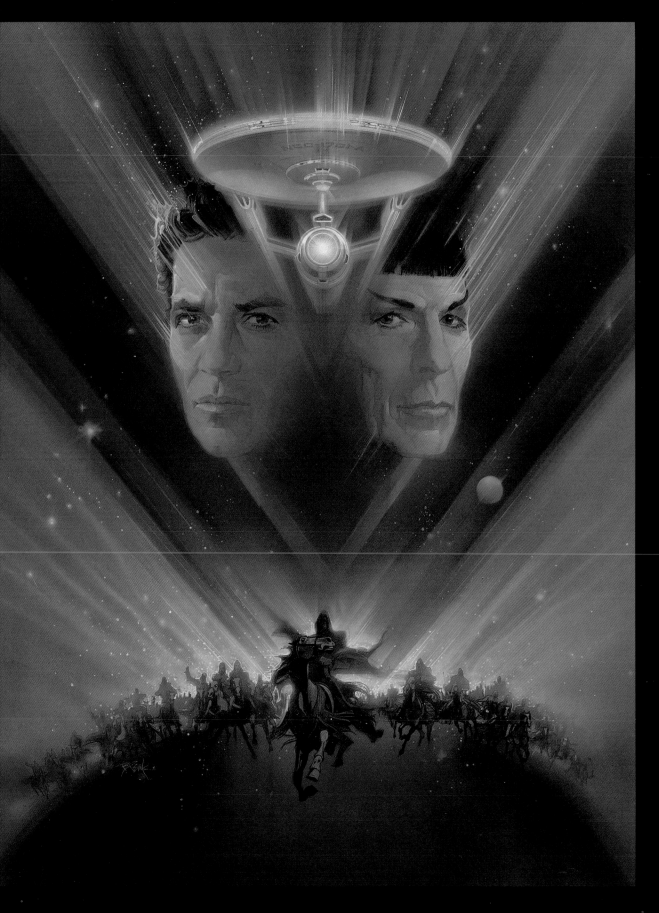

HARVEY KAHN
14 EAST 52 STREET NEW YORK, NY 10022

212 752-8490
FAX: 212-753-1721

BERNIE FUCH

HARVEY KAHN   212 752-84
14 EAST 52 STREET NEW YORK NY 10022

GERRY GERSTEN

HARVEY KAHN   212 752-8490

14 EAST 52 STREET NEW YORK, NY 10022   FAX: 212 753 1721

HANKINS+TEGENBORG

60 E. 42ND STREET NEW YORK, NY 10165

PHONE **212-867-8092** PHONE

F A X **212-949-1977** F A X

CALL FOR OUR NEW
64-PAGE CATALOG REPRESENTING:

RALPH BRILLHART	ALETA JENKS	DAN SNEBERGER
GEORGE BUSH	RICK JOHNSON	FRANK STEINER
JAMIE CAVALIERE	ULDIS KLAVINS	JEFF WALKER
MAC CONNER	RICHARD LAUTER	JOHN YOUSSI
GUY DEEL	SANDY KOSSIN	VINCE NATALE
JOHN TAYLOR DISMUKES	JOHN MAZZINI	TED SIZEMORE
BILL DODGE	NEAL McPHEETERS	DOREEN MINUTO
MARC ERICKSEN	CLIFF MILLER	MITZURA SALGIAN
GEORGE FERNANDEZ	ANDY POLLARD	KEN ROSENBERG
DAVID GAADT	WALTER RANE	BOB BERRAN
SERGIO GIOVINE	DON RODELL	KIRK REINERT
JIM GRIFFIN	HARRY SCHAARE	STEPHEN GARDNER
RAY HARVEY	BILL SCHMIDT	DANILO DUCAK
EDWIN HERDER	MIRO SINOVCIC	GARY BENNETT
MICHAEL HERRING	DIANE SIVAVEC	

DAN LAVIGNE

Freedom of the Press

BOB LAPSLEY

LARRY WINBORG

LYNN STEPHENS

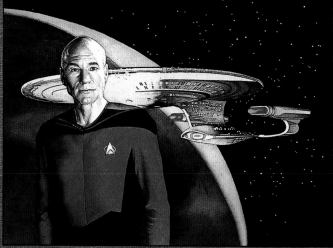

JACK DE GRAFFENRIED

represented by

BARNEY KANE & SID BUCK

566 7th Avenue, New York City 10018

212·221·8090

WALLY NEIBART

PHILIPPE RENAUDIN

ANN FOX

BILL THOMSON

ARTIST AT WORK...

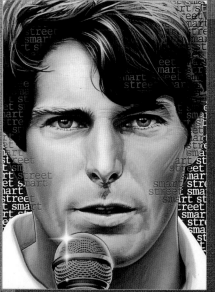

Warner Bros.

MGM/UA

EMPTY BEACH

Vestron

PLAY..

R. SCHEICHER

CENTRAL FLORIDA REGION of the SPORTS CAR CLUB OF AMERICA Presents the
1989 SOLO II CHAMPIONSHIP SERIES
AUTOCROSS!
DRIVE YOUR CAR TO THE LIMIT! SAFELY

BRIDGESTONE

GREG LEARY

SERVICE.

Images

MSIA Chart of the Realms

Heartfelt Foundation

DAVID **JARVIS** ILLUSTRATION

STUDIO
200 S. Banana River Boulevard
Cocoa Beach, Florida 32931
(407) 784•6263

W^mHARRISON

ILLUSTRATION

NEW YORK:
RENARD REPRESENTS

IF YOU HAVE GOOD NEWS, OR MONEY:
BILL HARRISON

212·490·2450
FAX 212·697·6828

708·232·7733
FAX 708·232·7741

TRUST ME

ROBERT FLORCZAK ILLUSTRATION

LOS ANGELES
MOZART
ORCHESTRA

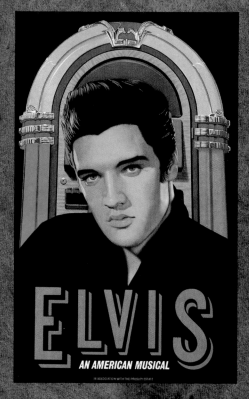

ELVIS
AN AMERICAN MUSICAL
IN ASSOCIATION WITH THE PRESLEY ESTATE

Represented by
RANDY PATE & ASSOC, INC.
(818) 985-8181 Fax: (818) 995-4566

THE
SOURCE

Color Separations by Graphic Arts Systems

BRYAN **HAYNES** ILLUSTRATION

Represented by
RANDY PATE & ASSOC, INC.
(818) 985-8181 Fax: (818) 995-4566

THE
SOURCE

JOHN **DISMUKES** ILLUSTRATION

Represented by: RANDY PATE & ASSOC, INC.   (818) 985-8181 Fax: (818) 995-4566

THE SOURCE

Color Separations by Graphic Arts Systems

KIMBLE

David Kimble
213 · 849 · 1576

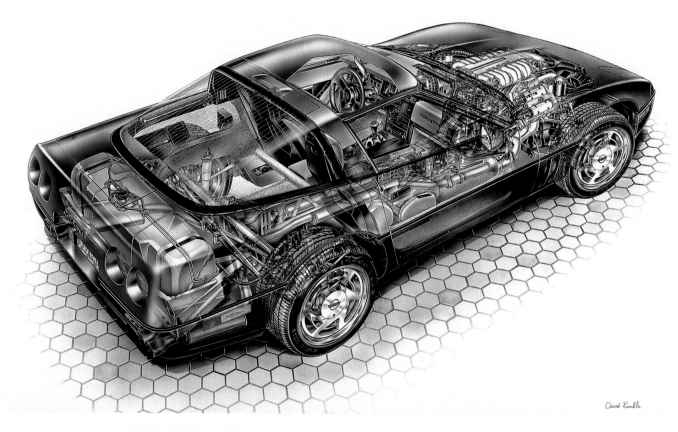

KIRSCH
R E P R E S E N T S
7316 Pyramid Dr., LA, CA 90046
213 651·3706

WACK

MCCLURE

Royce McClure

818 • 352 • 6900

KITCHELL

Joyce Kitchell
6 1 9 · 2 9 1 · 1 3 7 8

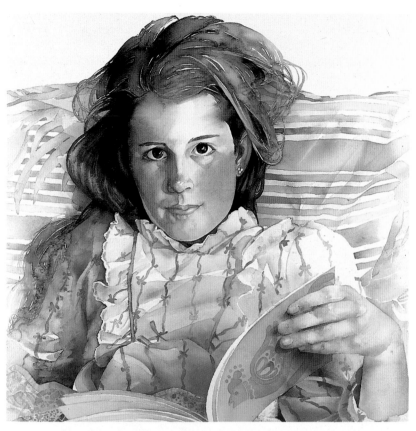

JOHNNA

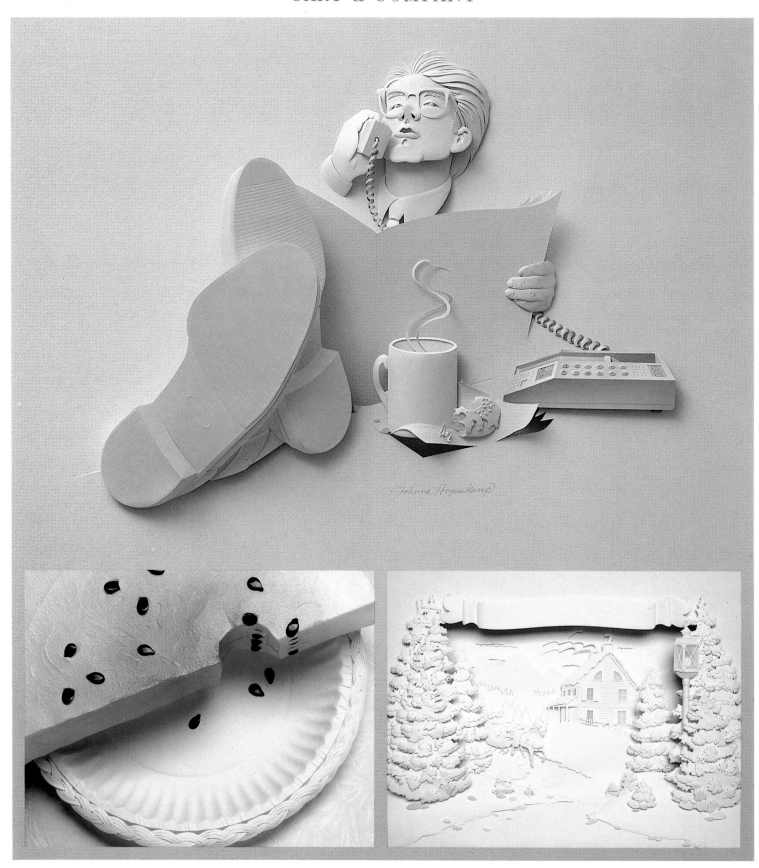

MIKE HODGES

404 • 296 • 9666

CHARLIE MITCHELL

REPRESENTED BY

CARY & COMPANY

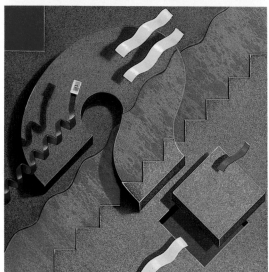

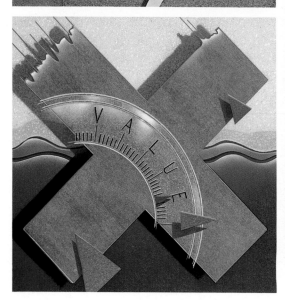

GREG OLSEN

CARY & COMPANY

REPERTORY

2 1 3 9 3 1 7 4 4 9

LORETTA GREER · ROB JACOBS

FAX 2 1 3 2 5 8 9 4 5 0

T O M C H R I S T O P H E R

Courtesy of the Charles Stark Draper Laboratories

STUDIO 718 278 4661

322

LINGTA KUNG

REPERTORY

2 1 3   9 3 1   7 4 4 9

LORETTA GREER • ROB JACOBS

FAX 213   258 9450

GLENDALE GALLERIA

K A Z   A I Z A W A

R E P E R T O R Y

2 1 3   9 3 1   7 4 4 9

LORETTA GREER • ROB JACOBS

FAX   213   258   9450

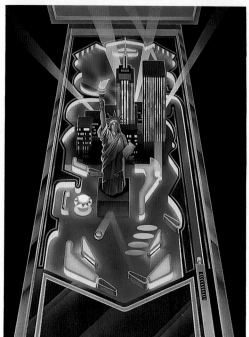

RICHARD ARRUDA

REPERTORY

2 1 3   9 3 1   7 4 4 9

LORETTA GREER • ROB JACOBS

F A X   2 1 3   2 5 8   9 4 5 0

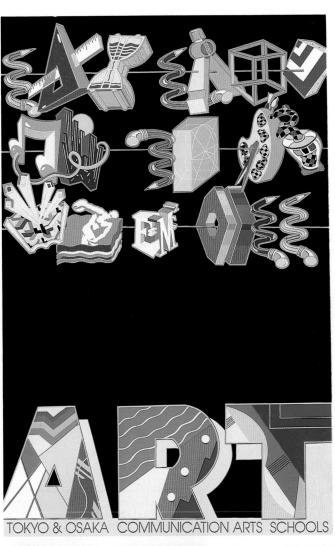

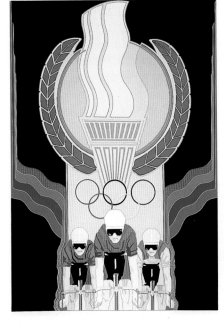

LAURIE PRIBBLE
ARTIST'S REPRESENTATIVE
818·574·0288   FAX 818·574·3940

Represented in San Francisco by
Kathy Braun Represents
(415) 775-3366

Represented in New York by
Sal Barracca & Assoc. Inc.
(212) 889-2400

JOHN HUXTABLE

1427 E. 4TH ST. #6   LOS ANGELES, CA 90033

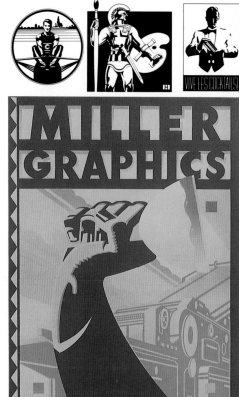

LAURIE PRIBBLE

ARTIST'S REPRESENTATIVE

818·574·0288   FAX 818·574·3940

WARREN CHANG

J A C K  M O L*L*O Y

2 1 2

D
A
N

P
I
C
A
S
S
O

KAREN KLUGLEIN

Represented by
Judy Mattelson
212-684-2974

RALSTON PURINA

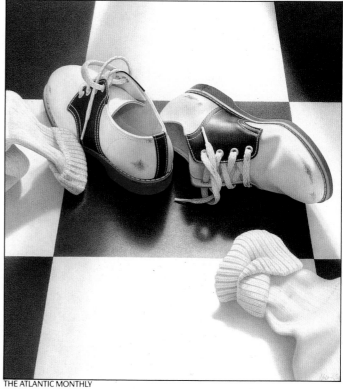

THE ATLANTIC MONTHLY

NESTLE

GLACIAL CONFECTIONS, INC.

UNITED DAIRY FARMERS

MIKASA

332

MARVIN MATTELSON

Represented by
Judy Mattelson
212-684-2974

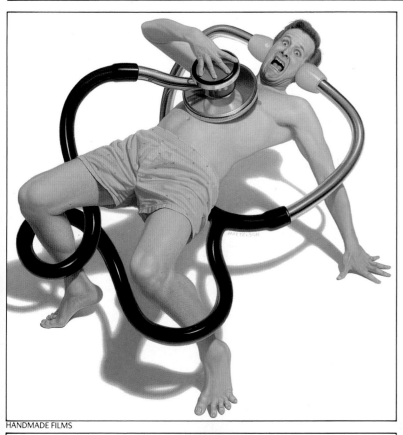

HANDMADE FILMS

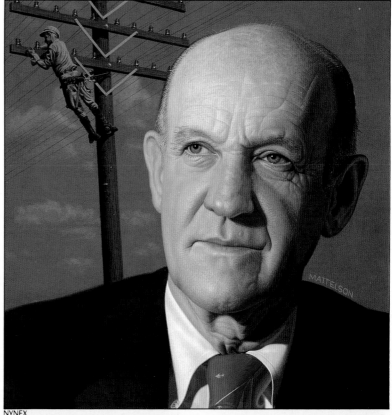

NYNEX

LINCOLN-MERCURY

TELARC

CBS RECORDS

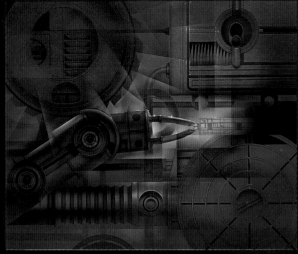

DON BRAUTIGAM

NORMAN WALKER

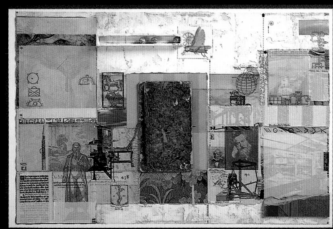

STEVE KARCHIN

ROBERT HEINDEL

MICHAEL DEAS

NORMAN ADAMS

FRED OTNES

MARK ENGLISH

MICHAEL DUDASH

DICK KREPEL

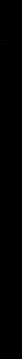

BILL ERLACHER ARTISTS ASSOCIATES ■ 211 EAST 51ST STREET ■ NEW YORK, NEW YORK 10022 ■ TELEPHONE (212) 755-13

BILL ERLACHER ARTISTS ASSOCIATE

FOLIO

IN THE U.S. CONTACT:
JENNIFER RODERICK
450 SEVENTH AVENUE
NEW YORK CITY 10123
212 268-1788
FAX: 629-5269

IN EUROPE CONTACT:
FOLIO
10 GATE STREET
LINCOLN'S INN FIELDS
LONDON, WC2-A3HP
01 242-9562
FAX: 01 242-1816

DAVID JUNIPER ————————————————

SYD BRAK ————————————————————

RAY WINDER ————————————————————

Il computer è il nocciolo. Bull vi dà anche la polpa.

Worldwide Information Systems

I frutti dell'informatica. Bull

FOLIO

JAMES MARSH

POVL WEBB

EAN TAYLOR

GEORGE UNDERWOOD

ANIMAL TESTING & COSMETICS

CRUEL/UNNECESSARY/REJECTED BY THE BODY SHOP

JC KNAFF

Aldridge Reps, Inc.
755 Virginia Avenue
Atlanta, Georgia 30306
(404) 872-7980
FAX: (404) 874 9681

Representing:
Chris Lewis

Samples also appear in American
Showcase volume 8, page 206; volume
9, page 219; volume 10, page 595;
volume 11, page 245; Volume 12, page
280.

Aldridge

Aldridge Reps, Inc.
755 Virginia Avenue
Atlanta, Georgia 30306
(404) 872-7980
FAX: (404) 874-9681

Representing:
Marcia Wetzel

Clients include Trousdell Design, Coca-Cola, Ogilvy & Mather, Southeastern Exposures.

Samples also appear in American Showcase Volume 11, page 246; Volume 12, page 282.

Aldridge

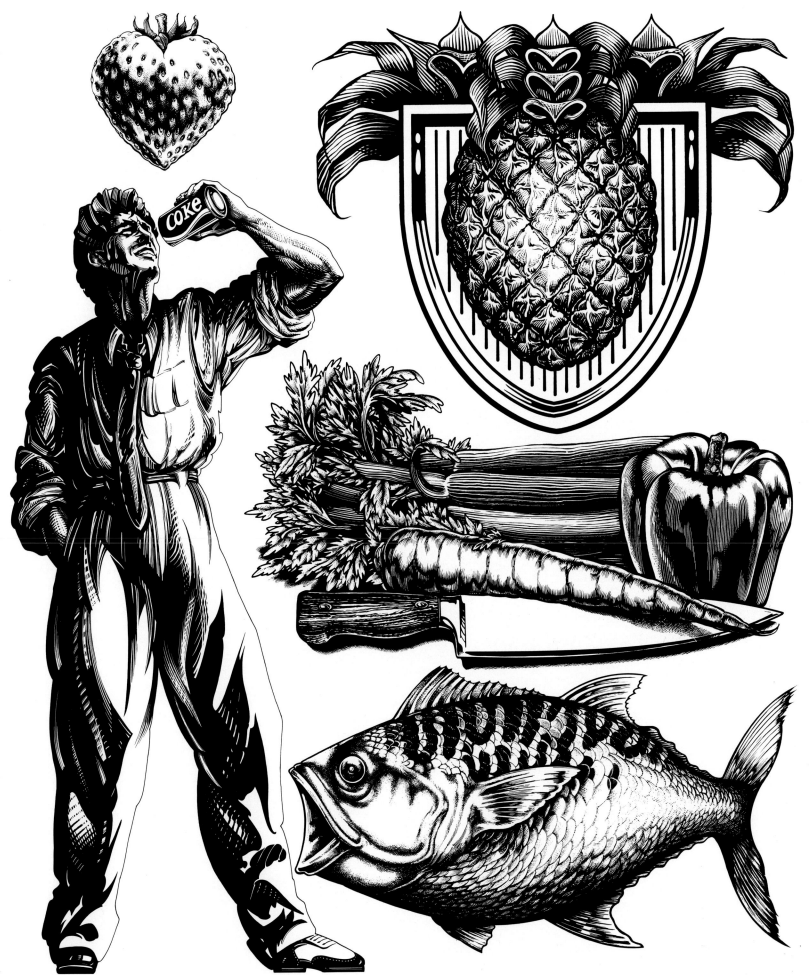

Aldridge Reps, Inc.
755 Virginia Avenue
Atlanta, Georgia 30306
(404) 872-7980
FAX: (404) 874-9681

Representing:
Thomas Gonzalez

Other samples appear in American Showcase Illustration volume II, page 244; volume 12, page 281 and the New Creative Illustration Book.

Aldridge

MCCANN ERICKSON/AD—DEB BERGER

SELF PROMOTION

Aldridge Reps, Inc.
755 Virginia Avenue
Atlanta, Georgia 30306
(404) 872-7980 • FAX: (404) 874-9681

Representing:
Carol H. Norby
(801) 756-1096

Aldridge

"WORD PERFECT" THE MAGAZINE

"IMPRINT" SOUTHERN BELL

"LAN TIMES" NOVELLE

Aldridge Reps, Inc.
755 Virginia Avenue
Atlanta, Georgia 30306
(404) 872-7980
FAX: (404) 874-9681

Representing:
Leslie Harris

Humor in two and three dimensions.
From concept to production.

Aldridge

Aldridge Reps, Inc.
755 Virginia Avenue
Atlanta, Georgia 30306
(404) 872-7980
FAX: (404) 874-9681

Representing:
Leslie Harris

Humor in two and three dimensions.
From concept to production.

Aldridge

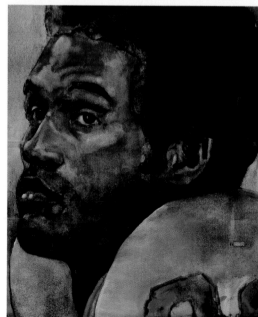

ARTCO

Illustrators'/Photographers' Representatives

The following 40 pages contain samples of some of the finest illustrators and sculptors in the country. They understand deadlines, work within budgets and are true professionals in every sense. This group of talented artists offers a wide variety of styles tied together by a common thread... excellence in technique and design. ARTCO represents...

Ed Acuna	**Bob Dacey**	**Kathy Jeffers**
Alexander & Turner	**Alan & Beau Daniels**	**Rick McCollum**
George Angelini	**Mort Drucker**	**John Jude Palencar**
Dan Brown	**Lisa Falkenstern**	**Marcel Rozenberg**
Alain Chang	**Ed Gazsi**	**Leslie Szabo**
Anne Cook	**Gary Glover**	**Sally Vitsky**
Jeff Cornell	**Lisa Henderling**	

If you would like to receive our ARTCO binder containing many more samples of each of our group, please give us a call or write.

In New York City:

ARTCO
232 Madison Avenue, Rm. 600
New York, N.Y. 10016
(212) 889-8777

From outside New York City:

ARTCO
227 Godfrey Road
Weston, Connecticut 06883
(203) 222-8777

ARTCO
Gail Thurm and Jeff Palmer

Representing:
Ed Acuna

Serving clients in New York City:
232 Madison Avenue, Suite 600
New York, New York 10016
(212) 889-8777 • FAX#: (212) 725-2210

Serving clients outside New York City:
227 Godfrey Road
Weston, Connecticut 06883
(203) 222-8777 • FAX#: (203) 454-9940

The Gallery

ARTCO
Gail Thurm and Jeff Palmer

Representing:
Alexander & Turner

Serving clients in New York City:
232 Madison Avenue, Suite 600
New York, New York 10016
(212) 889-8777 • FAX#: (212) 725-2210

Serving clients outside New York City:
227 Godfrey Road
Weston, Connecticut 06883
(203) 222-8777 • FAX#: (203) 454-9940

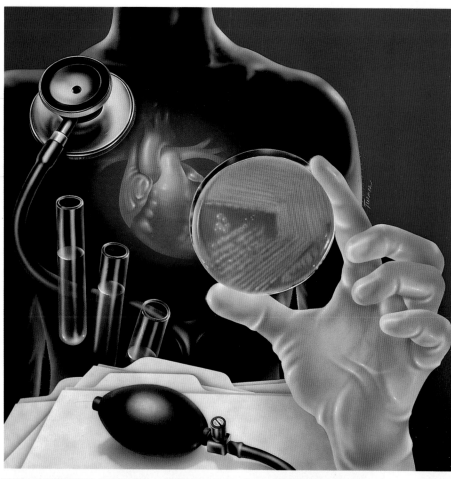

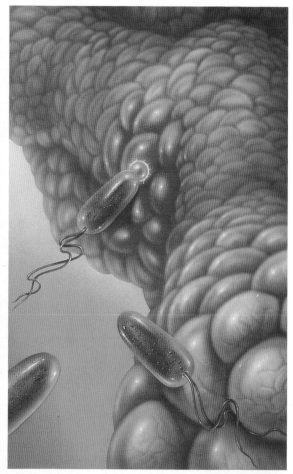

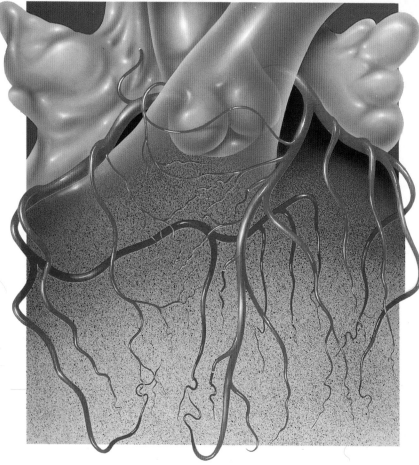

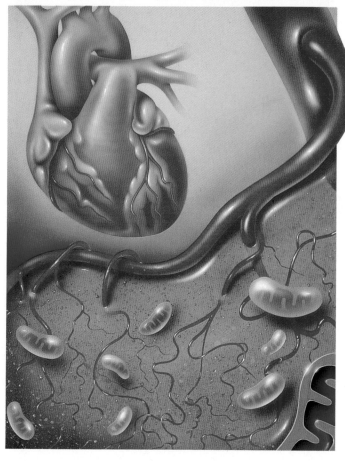

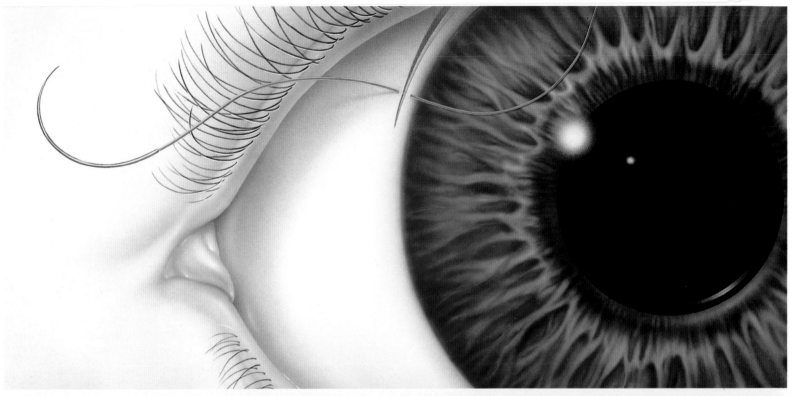

ARTCO
Gail Thurm and Jeff Palmer

Representing:
George Angelini

Serving clients in New York City:
232 Madison Avenue, Suite 600
New York, New York 10016
(212) 889-8777 • FAX#: (212) 725-2210

Serving clients outside New York City:
227 Godfrey Road
Weston, Connecticut 06883
(203) 222-8777 • FAX#: (203) 454-9940

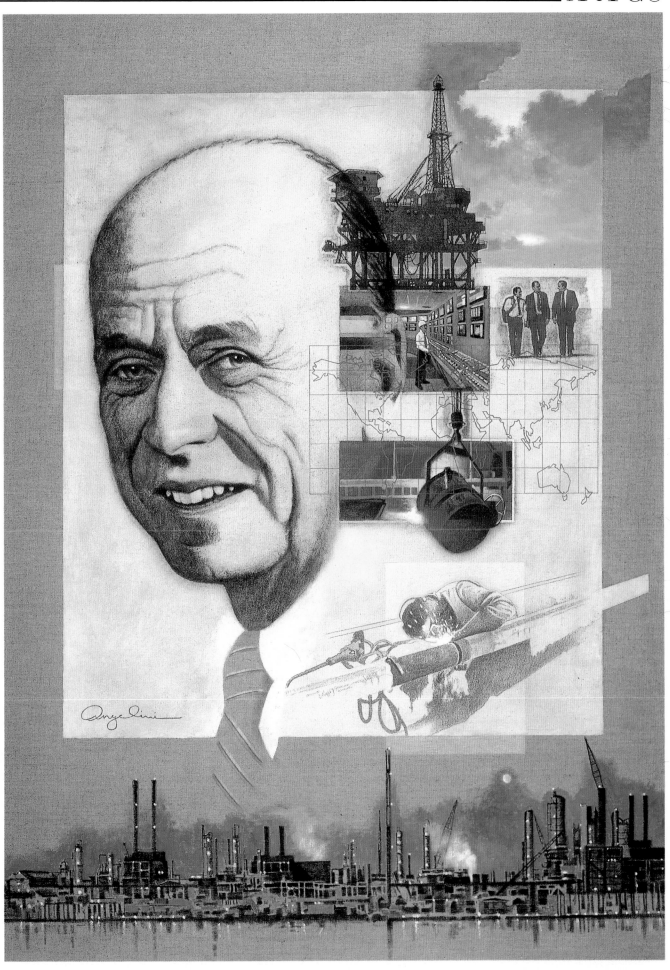

ARTCO
Gail Thurm and Jeff Palmer

Representing:
Dan Brown

Serving clients in New York City:
232 Madison Avenue, Suite 600
New York, New York 10016
(212) 889-8777 • FAX#: (212) 725-2210

Serving clients outside New York City:
227 Godfrey Road
Weston, Connecticut 06883
(203) 222-8777 • FAX#: (203) 454-9940

ARTCO

Gail Thurm and Jeff Palmer

Representing:
Alain Chang

Serving clients in New York City:
232 Madison Avenue, Suite 600
New York, New York 10016
(212) 889-8777 • FAX#: (212) 725-2210

Serving clients outside New York City:
227 Godfrey Road
Weston, Connecticut 06883
(203) 222-8777 • FAX#: (203) 454-9940

In San Francisco:
Lydia Lawrence Represents
(415) 921-2415

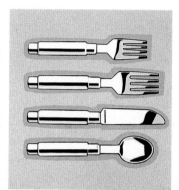

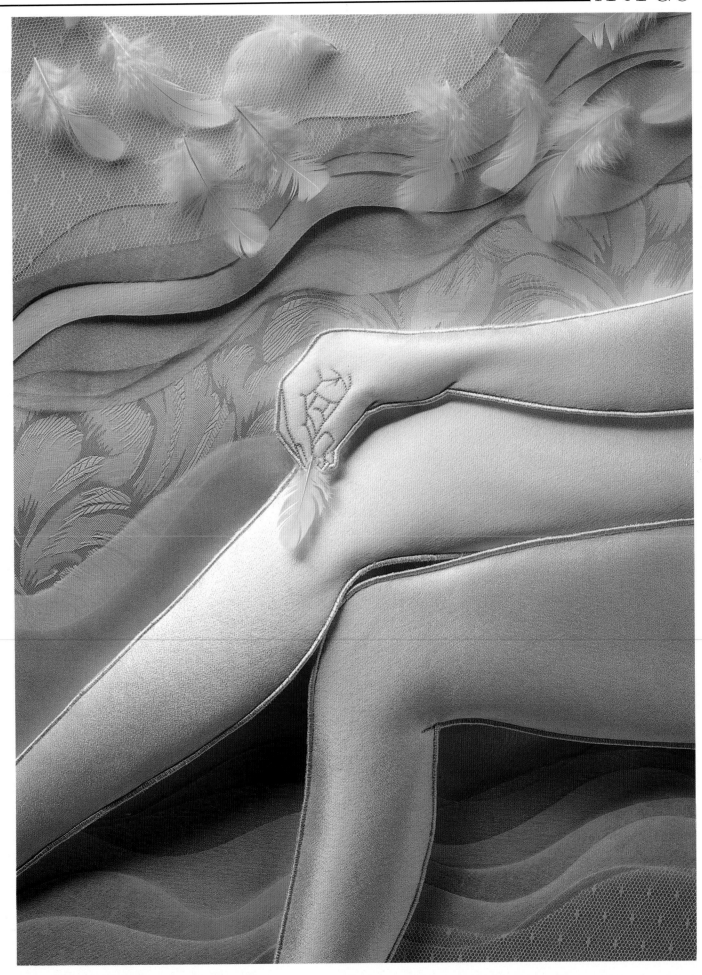

ARTCO
Gail Thurm and Jeff Palmer

Representing:
Jeff Cornell

Serving clients in New York City:
232 Madison Avenue, Suite 600
New York, New York 10016
(212) 889-8777 • FAX#: (212) 725-2210

Serving clients outside New York City:
227 Godfrey Road
Weston, Connecticut 06883
(203) 222-8777 • FAX#: (203) 454-9940

ARTCO
Gail Thurm and Jeff Palmer

Representing:
Bob Dacey

Serving clients in New York City:
232 Madison Avenue, Suite 600
New York, New York 10016
(212) 889-8777 • FAX#: (212) 725-2210

Serving clients outside New York City:
227 Godfrey Road
Weston, Connecticut 06883
(203) 222-8777 • FAX#: (203) 454-9940

ARTCO
Gail Thurm and Jeff Palmer

Representing:
Alan Daniels
Beau Daniels

Serving clients in New York City:
232 Madison Avenue, Suite 600
New York, New York 10016
(212) 889-8777 • FAX#: (212) 725-2210

Serving clients outside New York City:
227 Godfrey Road
Weston, Connecticut 06883
(203) 222-8777 • FAX#: (203) 454-9940

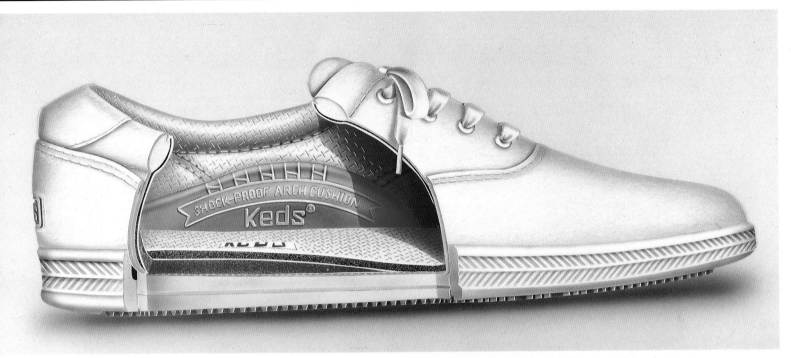

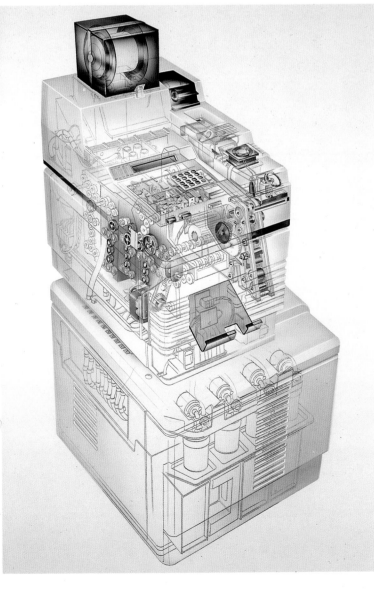

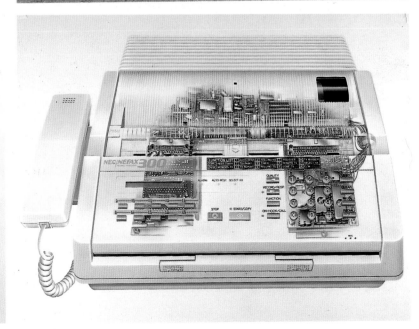

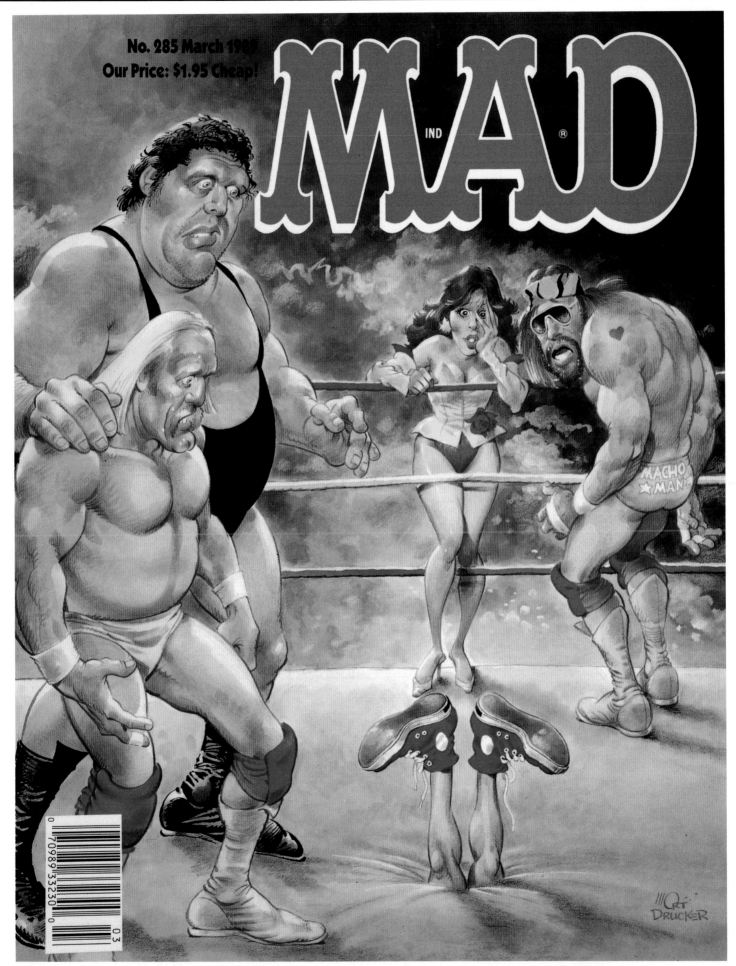

No. 285 March 1989
Our Price: $1.95 Cheap!

MAD

0 70989 33230 0
03

ARTCO
Gail Thurm and Jeff Palmer

Representing:
Lisa Falkenstern

Serving clients in New York City:
232 Madison Avenue, Suite 600
New York, New York 10016
(212) 889-8777 • FAX#: (212) 725-2210

Serving clients outside New York City:
227 Godfrey Road
Weston, Connecticut 06883
(203) 222-8777 • FAX#: (203) 454-9940

ARTCO
Gail Thurm and Jeff Palmer

Representing:
Ed Gazsi

Serving clients in New York City:
232 Madison Avenue, Suite 600
New York, New York 10016
(212) 889-8777 • FAX#: (212) 725-2210

Serving clients outside New York City:
227 Godfrey Road
Weston, Connecticut 06883
(203) 222-8777 • FAX#: (203) 454-9940

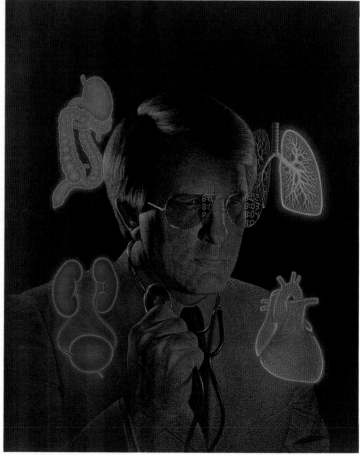

ARTCO
Gail Thurm and Jeff Palmer

Representing:
Lisa Henderling

Serving clients in New York City:
232 Madison Avenue, Suite 600
New York, New York 10016
(212) 889-8777 • FAX#: (212) 725-2210

Serving clients outside New York City:
227 Godfrey Road
Weston, Connecticut 06883
(203) 222-8777 • FAX#: (203) 454-9940

henderlina

ARTCO
Gail Thurm and Jeff Palmer

Representing:
Kathy Jeffers

Serving clients in New York City:
232 Madison Avenue, Suite 600
New York, New York 10016
(212) 889-8777 • FAX#: (212) 725-2210

Serving clients outside New York City:
227 Godfrey Road
Weston, Connecticut 06883
(203) 222-8777 • FAX#: (203) 454-9940

Dimensional illustration in clay

ARTCO
Gail Thurm and Jeff Palmer

Representing:
Rick McCollum

Serving clients in New York City:
232 Madison Avenue, Suite 600
New York, New York 10016
(212) 889-8777 • FAX#: (212) 725-2210

Serving clients outside New York City:
227 Godfrey Road
Weston, Connecticut 06883
(203) 222-8777 • FAX#: (203) 454-9940

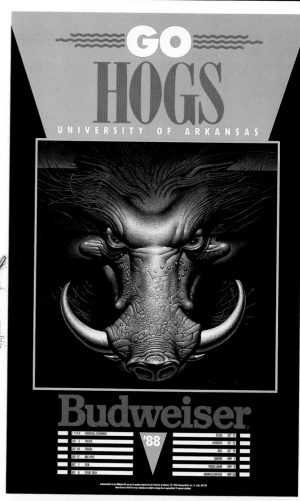

ARTCO
Gail Thurm and Jeff Palmer

Representing:
Leslie Szabo

Serving clients in New York City:
232 Madison Avenue, Suite 600
New York, New York 10016
(212) 889-8777 • FAX#: (212) 725-2210

Serving clients outside New York City:
227 Godfrey Road
Weston, Connecticut 06883
(203) 222-8777 • FAX#: (203) 454-9940

ARTCO
Gail Thurm and Jeff Palmer

Representing:
Sally Vitsky

Serving clients in New York City:
232 Madison Avenue, Suite 600
New York, New York 10016
(212) 889-8777 • FAX#: (212) 725-2210

Serving clients outside New York City:
227 Godfrey Road
Weston, Connecticut 06883
(203) 222-8777 • FAX#: (203) 454-9940

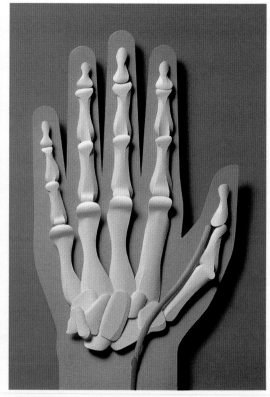

Photography: Lee Salsbery

ALASKA

Alaska Artists Guild
PO Box 101888
Anchorage, AK 99510
(907) 277-1962

ARIZONA

Arizona Artist Guild
8912 North Fourth Street
Phoenix, AZ 85020
(602) 944-9713

CALIFORNIA

Advertising Club of Los Angeles
3600 Wilshire Boulevard, Suite 432
Los Angeles, CA 90010
(213) 382-1228

APA Los Angeles, Inc.
7201 Melrose Avenue
Los Angeles, CA 90046
(213) 935-7283

Art Directors and Artists Club
2791 24th Street
Sacramento, CA 95818
(916) 731-7532

Book Club of California
312 Sutter Street, Suite 510
San Francisco, CA 94108
(415) 781-7532

Los Angeles Advertising Women
5000 Van Nuys Boulevard, Suite 400
Sherman Oaks, CA 91403
(818) 995-7338

San Francisco Art Directors Club
2757 16th Street, Box 277
San Francisco, CA 94103
(415) 387-4040

Society of Illustrators of Los Angeles
5000 Van Nuys Boulevard, Suite 400
Sherman Oaks, CA 91403
(818) 784-0588

Society of Motion Pictures & TV Art Directors
14724 Ventura Boulevard, Penthouse #4
Sherman Oaks, CA 91403
(818) 905-0599

Visual Artists Association
5364 Venice Boulevard
Los Angeles, CA 90019
(213) 933-7199

Western Art Directors Club
PO Box 996
Palo Alto, CA 94302
(415) 321-4196

Women's Graphic Center
The Woman's Building
1727 North Spring Street
Los Angeles, CA 90012
(213) 222-5101

COLORADO

Art Directors Club of Denver
1900 Grant Street, Suite 1130
Denver, CO 80203
(303) 830-7888

International Design Conference in Aspen
1000 North 3rd
Aspen, CO 81612
(303) 925-2257

CONNECTICUT

Connecticut Art Directors Club
PO Box 639
Avon, CT 06001
(203) 651-0886

DISTRICT OF COLUMBIA

American Advertising Federation
1400 K Street NW, Suite 1000
Washington, DC 20005
(202) 898-0089

American Institute of Architects
1735 New York Avenue, NW
Washington, DC 20006
(202) 626-7300

Art Directors Club of Washington, DC
1015 20th Street NW, Suite M100
Washington, DC 20036
(202) 955-5775

NEA: Design Arts Program
1100 Pennsylvania Avenue, NW
Washington, DC 20506
(202) 682-5437

GEORGIA

Art Directors Club of Atlanta
125 Bennett Street, NW
Atlanta, GA 30309
(404) 352-8726

Atlanta Art Papers, Inc.
PO Box 77348
Atlanta, GA 30357
(404) 588-1837

Creative Arts Guild
PO Box 375
Dalton, GA 30722
(404) 278-0168

Graphic Artists Guild
PO Box 8178
Atlanta, GA 30306
(404) 473-8620

continued on page 413

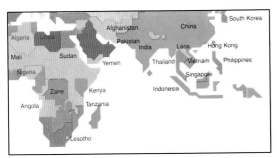

FORTUNE

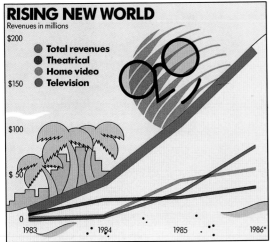

CHANNELS

AT&T

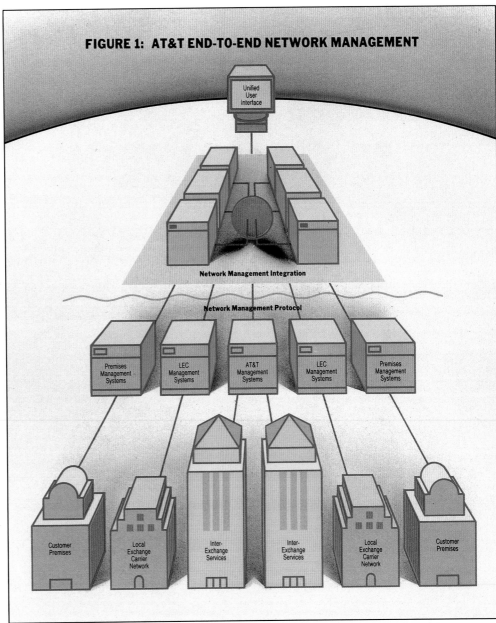

AT&T

AMERICAN JOURNAL OF NURSING CO.

RODALE PRESS

INSURANCE INFORMATION INSTITUTE

Darwin Bahm
6 Jane Street
New York, New York 10014
(212) 989-7074
(212) 627-0863 24 hour FAX

Representing:
John Thompson

Bob Bahm
(216) 398-1338

Darwin Bahm
6 Jane Street
New York, New York 10014
(212) 989-7074
(212) 627-0863 24 hour FAX

Representing:
Joan Landis

Bob Bahm
(216) 398-1338

**Ceci Bartels
Associates**
1913 Park
St. Louis, Missouri 63104
(314) 241-4014 STL
(212) 912-1877 NY
(312) 786-1560 CHIC
FAX: (314) 241-9028

LET US MAKE YOU A HERO.

We can make you a hero by being your personal art rep. We can help you gain market share for your clients. Win awards for your agency. And get you a big, fat raise. We will not only save you the time and energy it takes to find the right talent, we will help guide your job through so that you'll get on time, on budget delivery. We represent only the best. And the most important person we represent is you. So, perform an heroic act. Pick up the telephone and give us a call.

CECI BARTELS
ASSOCIATES
REPRESENTS
THESE TOP
ILLUSTRATORS,
PHOTOGRAPHERS
AND DIRECTORS.

*Jim Arndt
Bill Bruning
Justin Carroll
Cat Pak*

*Gary Ciccarelli
Bob Ebel
Paul Elledge
Mark Fredrickson
Frank Fruzyna
Stephen Grohe
Hero Pak
Keith Kasnot
Leland Klanderman
Shannon Kriegshauser
Greg MacNair
Pete Mueller
Adam Niklewicz*

*Jim Olvera
Kevin Pope
Guy Porfirio
Jean Probert
BB Sams
Todd Schorr
Jay Silverman
Terry Sirrell
T.P. Speer
Greg Stroube
Wayne Watford
Lin Wilson
Ted Wright*

Ceci Bartels Associates

1913 Park
St. Louis, Missouri 63104
(314) 241-4014 STL
(212) 912-1877 NY
(312) 786-1560 CHIC
FAX: (314) 241-9028

Representing:
Justin Carroll

**Ceci Bartels
Associates**

1913 Park
St. Louis, Missouri 63104
(314) 241-4014 STL
(212) 912-1877 NY
(312) 786-1560 CHIC
FAX: (314) 241-9028

Representing:
Jean Probert

Ceci Bartels Associates
1913 Park
St. Louis, Missouri 63104
(314) 241-4014 STL
(212) 912-1877 NY
(312) 786-1560 CHIC
FAX: (314) 241-9028

Representing:
Shannon Kriegshauser

**Ceci Bartels
Associates**
1913 Park
St. Louis, Missouri 63104
(314) 241-4014 STL
(212) 912-1877 NY
(312) 786-1560 CHIC
FAX: (314) 241-9028

Representing:
Bill Bruning

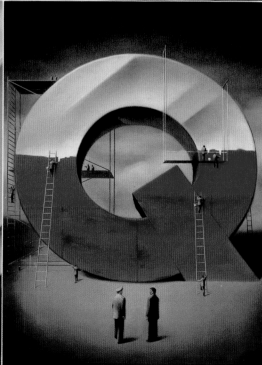

Ceci Bartels
Associates
1913 Park
St. Louis, Missouri 63104
(314) 241-4014 STL
(212) 912-1877 NY
(312) 786-1560 CHIC
FAX: (314) 241-9028

Representing:
Mark Fredrickson

**Ceci Bartels
Associates**
1913 Park
St. Louis, Missouri 63104
(314) 241-4014 STL
(212) 912-1877 NY
(312) 786-1560 CHIC
FAX: (314) 241-9028

Representing:
Leland Klanderman

**Ceci Bartels
Associates**
1913 Park
St. Louis, Missouri 63104
(314) 241-4014 STL
(212) 912-1877 NY
(312) 786-1560 CHIC
FAX: (314) 241-9028

Representing:
Guy Porfirio

**Ceci Bartels
Associates**
1913 Park
St. Louis, Missouri 63104
(314) 241-4014 STL
(212) 912-1877 NY
(312) 786-1560 CHIC
FAX: (314) 241-9028

Representing:
Greg MacNair

Ceci Bartels Associates
1913 Park
St. Louis, Missouri 63104
(314) 241-4014 STL
(212) 912-1877 NY
(312) 786-1560 CHIC
FAX: (314) 241-9028

Representing:
Ted Wright

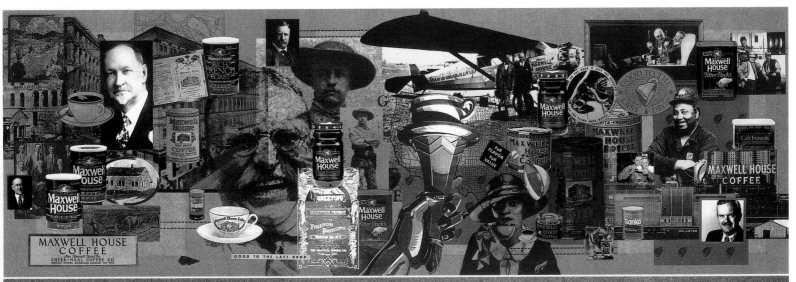

Ceci Bartels Associates

1913 Park
St. Louis, Missouri 63104
(314) 241-4014 STL
(212) 912-1877 NY
(312) 786-1560 CHIC
FAX: (314) 241-9028

Representing:
Kevin Pope

Ed and Skeeter rounding up the cows.

Monroe could slice the catsup, but he just couldn't cut the mustard.

Seven-alarm chili

Trying to iron all the bugs out.

Hello Mona, This is Your Life!

Where Life rears its Ugly Head, U.S.A.

Where Money doesn't grow on trees.

Heyyyyy... Not Bad!!

A wolf in Sheep's Clothing.

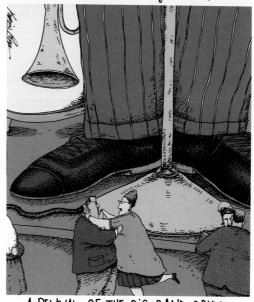

A Revival of the Big Band Sound.

Myron had that... well, you know...
Electric Personality

**Ceci Bartels
Associates**
1913 Park
St. Louis, Missouri 63104
(314) 241-4014 STL
(212) 912-1877 NY
(312) 786-1560 CHIC
FAX: (314) 241-9028

Representing:
Wayne Watford

401

Bookmakers Ltd.
25 Sylvan Road South
Westport, Connecticut 06880
(203) 226-4293
FAX: (203) 226-4294

Representing:
George Guzzi

Clients Include: NASA, U.S. Air Force,
U.S. Coast Guard, U.S. Postal Service,
NBC Seagrams' Distillers, Ford Motor
Co., American Express, McDonald's,
Grumman Aircraft, Readers' Digest,
Redbook, Cosmopolitan, American
Heritage, Motorboat, Sail, WORLD Book,
Grosset & Dunlap, Paramount Pictures.

BOOKMAKERS

Bookmakers Ltd.
25 Sylvan Road South
Westport, Connecticut 06880
(203) 226-4293
FAX: (203) 226-4294

Representing:
Steve Botts
Dick Smolinski
Lydia Halverson
Steve McInturff

Lydia Halverson

Steve Botts

Dick Smolinski

Steve McInturff

Bookmakers Ltd.
25 Sylvan Road South
Westport, Connecticut 06880
(203) 226-4293
FAX: (203) 226-4294

Representing:
Judith A.R. Lombardi
Marsha Serafin
Kathy McCord
David Neuhaus

Judith A. R. Lombardi

Kathleen McCord

Marsha Serafin

David Neuhaus

Bookmakers Ltd.
25 Sylvan Road South
Westport, Connecticut 06880
(203) 226-4293
FAX: (203) 226-4294

Representing:
Sharon Steuer
David Bolinsky
Keith Lo Bue

BOOKMAKERS

Sharon Steuer   *Illustrations handpainted on the computer for print and broadcast.*

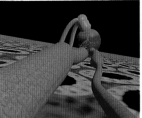

Keith Lo Bue   *Airbrush illustration.*

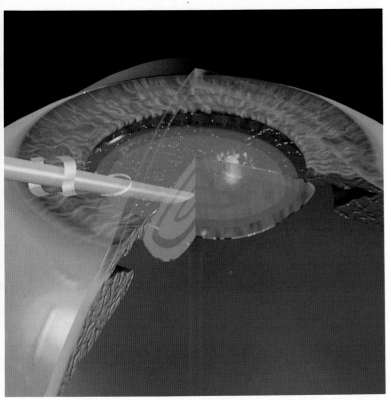

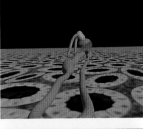

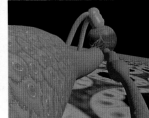

David Bolinsky   *State of the art Wavefront Technologies 3-D software for print and animation.*
Specializing in medical and pharmaceutical applications.

**John Brewster/
Creative Services**
597 Riverside Avenue
Westport, Connecticut 06880
(203) 226-4724 • FAX (203) 454-9904

Representing:
Al Weston

In the Detroit area call:
AW Graphics
3476 Newgate Road
Troy, Michigan 48084
(313) 642-9172

John Brewster/
Creative Services
597 Riverside Avenue
Westport, Connecticut 06880
(203) 226-4724 • FAX (203) 454-9904

Representing:
Lane DuPont

JBCS

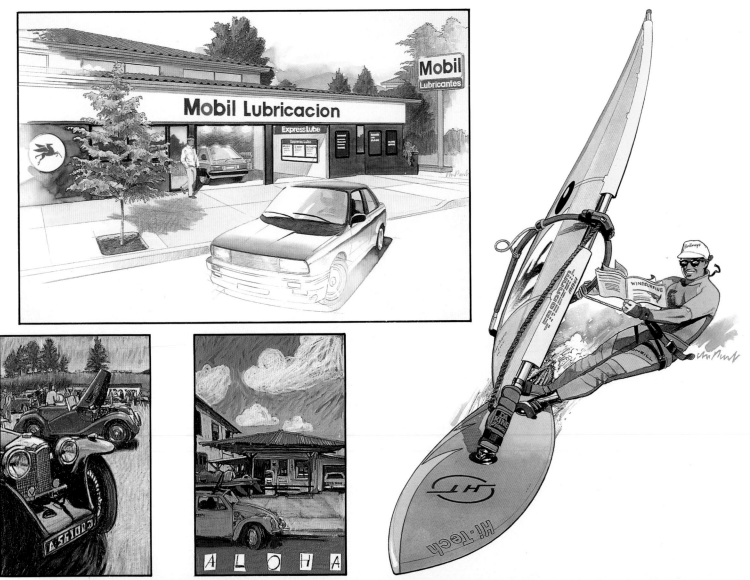

**John Brewster/
Creative Services**

597 Riverside Avenue
Westport, Connecticut 06880
(203) 226-4724 • FAX (203) 454-9904

Representing:
Steven Stroud

JBCS

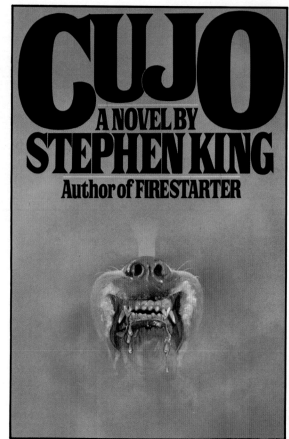

**John Brewster/
Creative Services**
597 Riverside Avenue
Westport, Connecticut 06880
(203) 226-4724 • FAX (203) 454-9904

Representing:
Nan Parson

In New York Call:
(212) 682-2462 American Artists

JBCS

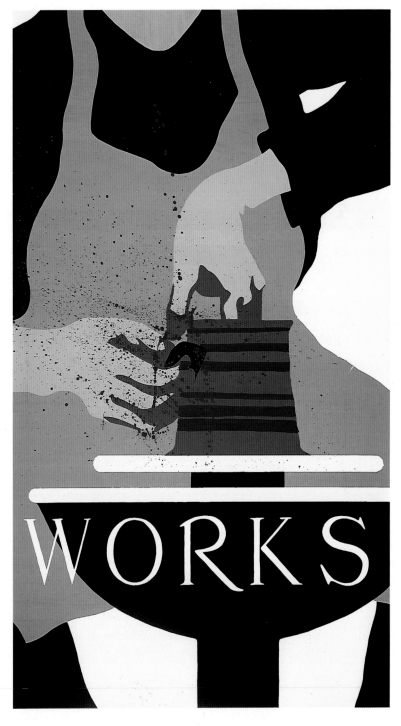

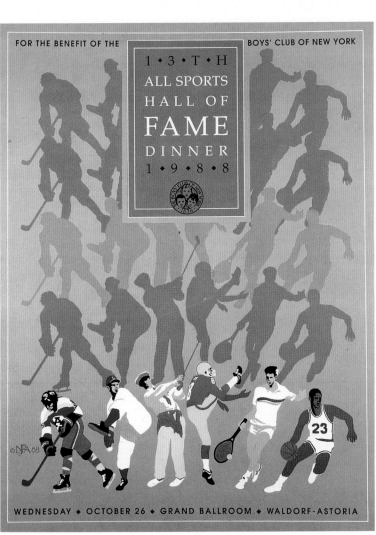

**John Brewster/
Creative Services**

597 Riverside Avenue
Westport, Connecticut 06880
(203) 226-4724 • FAX (203) 454-9904

Representing:
Mike Brent

JBCS

**John Brewster/
Creative Services**
597 Riverside Avenue
Westport, Connecticut 06880
(203) 226-4724 • FAX (203) 454-9904

Representing:
Alan Neider

In New York City call:
Bill and Maurine Klimt
15 West 72nd Street
New York, New York 10023
(212) 799-2231

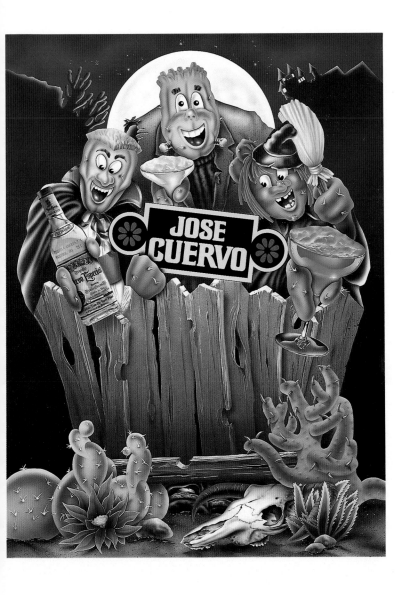

continued from page 386

ILLINOIS

Artists Guild of Chicago
410 North Michigan Avenue
Lower Level
Chicago, IL 60611
(312) 951-8252

Chicago Society of Artists, Inc.
1142 West Morse Avenue
Chicago, IL 60626
(312) 764-6119

Institute of Business Designers
341 Merchandise Mart
Chicago, IL 60654
(312) 467-1950

Society of Typographic Arts
233 East Ontario Street, Suite 500
Chicago, IL 60611
(312) 787-2018

Women in Design
2 North Riverside Plaza, Suite 2400
Chicago, IL 60606
(312) 648-1874

INDIANA

Advertising Club of Indianapolis
3833 North Meridian
Suite 305 B
Indianapolis, IN 46208
(317) 631-2000

IOWA

Art Guild of Burlington
Arts for Living Center
PO Box 5
Burlington, IA 52601
(319) 754-8069

KENTUCKY

Davidson County Art Guild
224 South Main Street
Lexington, KY 27292
(704) 249-2742

MASSACHUSETTS

Boston Visual Artists Union
77 North Washington Street, 3rd Floor
Boston, MA 02114
(617) 227-3076

Creative Club of Boston
155 Massachusetts Avenue
Boston, MA 02115
(617) 536-8999

Center for Design of Industrial Schedules
221 Longwood Avenue
Boston, MA 02115
(617) 734-2163

Graphic Artists Guild
PO Box 1454-GMF
Boston, MA 02205
(617) 451-5362

Guild of Boston Artists
162 Newbury Street
Boston, MA 02116
(617) 536-7660

Society of Environmental Graphics Designers
47 Third Street
Cambridge, MA 02141
(617) 577-8225

MICHIGAN

Creative Advertising Club of Detroit
c/o Josephine LaLonde
30400 Van Dyke
Warren, MI 48093

Michigan Guild of Artists and Artisans
118 North Fourth Avenue
Ann Arbor, MI 48104
(313) 662-3382

MINNESOTA

Advertising Federation of Minnesota
4248 Park Glen Road
Minneapolis, MN 55416
(612) 929-1445

MISSOURI

Advertising Center of Greater St. Louis
440 Mansion House Center
St. Louis, MO 63102
(314) 231-4185

Advertising Club of Kansas City
1 Ward Parkway Center, Suite 102
Kansas City, MO 64112
(816) 753-4088

Kansas City Art Directors Club
Westport Station
PO Box 10022
Kansas City, MO 64111
(816) 561-4301

NEW JERSEY

Federated Art Associations of New Jersey, Inc.
PO Box 2195
Westfield, NJ 07090
(201) 232-7623

Point-of-Purchase Advertising Institute
66 North Van Brunt Street
Englewood, NJ 07631
(201) 894-8899

NEW YORK

The Advertising Club of New York
155 East 55th Street
New York, NY 10022
(212) 935-8080
continued on page 434

Nancy Bruck
& Eileen Moss
(212) 980-8061
(212) 645-1547

Representing:
Warren Gebert

**Nancy Bruck
& Eileen Moss**
(212) 645-1547
(212) 980-8061

Representing:
Pamela Patrick

**Nancy Bruck
& Eileen Moss**
(212) 645-1547
(212) 980-8061

Representing
Lionsgate

Nancy Bruck
& Eileen Moss

(212) 980-8061
(212) 645-1547

Representing
Joel Peter Johnson

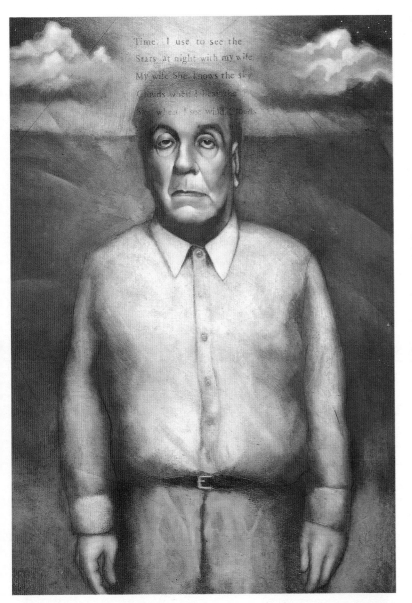

**Nancy Bruck
& Eileen Moss**
(212) 980-8061
(212) 645-1547

Representing:
Scott Pollack

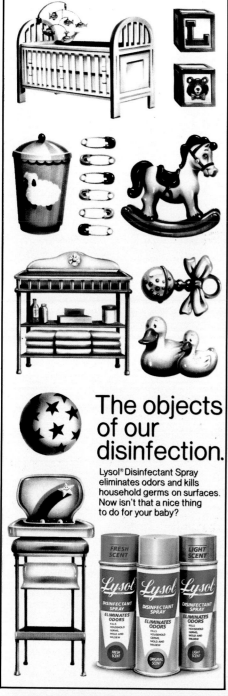

The objects
of our
disinfection.

Lysol® Disinfectant Spray
eliminates odors and kills
household germs on surfaces.
Now isn't that a nice thing
to do for your baby?

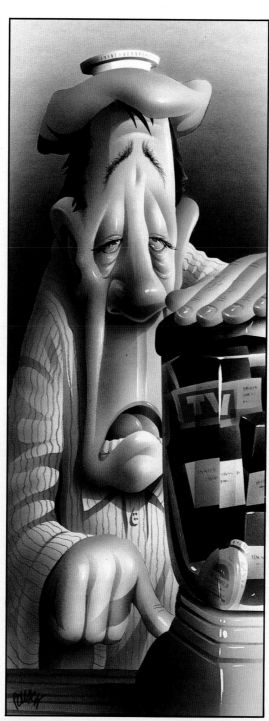

**Nancy Bruck
& Eileen Moss**
(212) 980-8061
(212) 645-1547

Representing:
Scott Pollack

Carol Chislovsky Inc.
853 Broadway, Suite #1201
New York, New York 10003
(212) 677-9100
FAX: (212) 353-0954

SANDRA SHAP

RANDY SOUTH

Carol Chislovsky Inc.
853 Broadway, Suite #1201
New York, New York 10003
(212) 677-9100
FAX: (212) 353-0954

ED SCARISBRICK

STEVE GRAY

C.A. TRACHOK

Carol Chislovsky Inc.
853 Broadway, Suite #1201
New York, New York 10003
(212) 677-9100
FAX: (212) 353-0954

KEN GRANING

JON CONRAD

NIGHTHAWK STUDIO

Carol Chislovsky Inc.
853 Broadway, Suite #1201
New York, New York 10003
(212) 677-9100
FAX: (212) 353-0954

RUSSELL COBANE

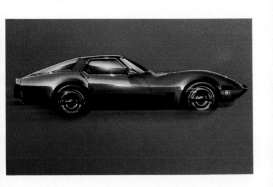

Split.

MARK HERMAN

IGNACIO GOMEZ

Carol Chislovsky Inc.
853 Broadway, Suite #1201
New York, New York 10003
(212) 677-9100
FAX: (212) 353-0954

JOE LAPINSKI

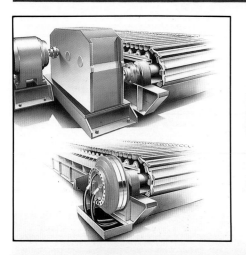

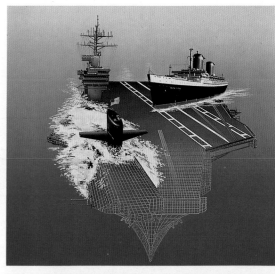

CHUCK SCHMIDT

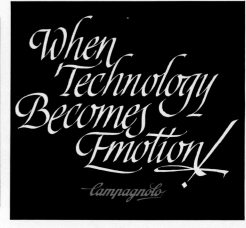

JULIE PACE

Creative Freelancers Management, Inc.

West 45th Street
New York, New York 10036
(212) 398-9540

Representing:
Mary O'Keefe Young

Creative Freelancers Management, Inc.
62 West 45th Street
New York, New York 10036
(212) 398-9540

Representing:
John Edens

**Creative Freelancers
Management, Inc.**
62 West 45th Street
New York, New York 10036
(212) 398-9540

Representing:
Chet Jezierski

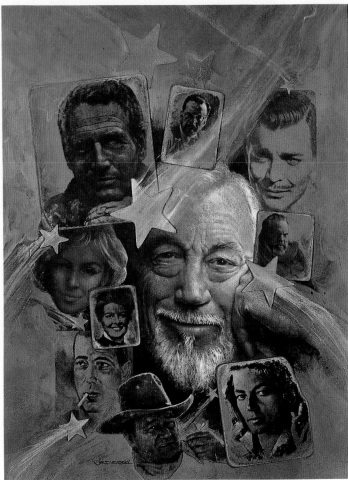

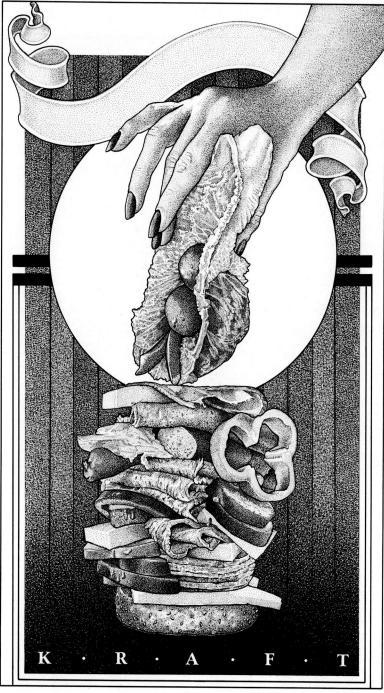

Creative Freelancers Management, Inc.
62 West 45th Street
New York, New York 10036
(212) 398-9540

Representing:
Anne Feiza

Creative Freelancers Management, Inc.
62 West 45th Street
New York, New York 10036
(212) 398-9540

Representing:
Joanna Roy

Joanna Roy

Creative Freelancers Management, Inc.
62 West 45th Street
New York, New York 10036
(212) 398-9540

Representing:
Greg Fitzhugh

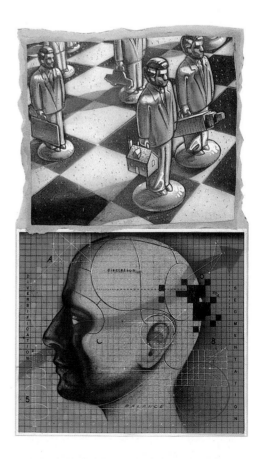

**Creative Freelancers
Management, Inc.**
62 West 45th Street
New York, New York 10036
(212) 398-9540

Representing:
Glen Schofield

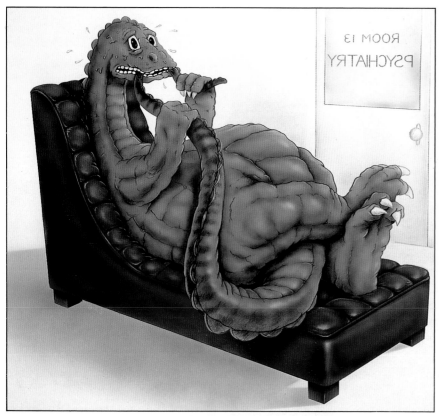

Creative Freelancers Management, Inc.
62 West 45th Street
New York, New York 10036
(212) 398-9540

Representing:
Steve Sullivan

continued from page 413

The Advertising Council, Inc.
825 Third Avenue
New York, NY 10022
(212) 758-0400

APA
Advertising Photographers of America, Inc.
27 West 20th Street, Room 601
New York, NY 10011
(212) 807-0399

Advertising Production Club of N.Y.
60 East 42nd Street, Suite 1130
New York, NY 10165
(212) 983-6042

Advertising Typographers Association of America, Inc.
Two Penn Plaza, Suite 1070
New York, NY 10121
(212) 629-3232

Advertising Women of New York Foundation, Inc.
153 East 57th Street
New York, NY 10022
(212) 593-1950

A.A.A.A.
American Association of Advertising Agencies
666 Third Avenue
New York, NY 10017
(212) 682-2500

American Booksellers Association, Inc.
137 West 25th Street
New York, NY 10001
(212) 463-8450

American Council for the Arts
1285 Avenue of the Americas
Third Floor
New York, NY 10019
(212) 245-4510

The American Institute of Graphic Arts
1059 Third Avenue, 3rd Floor
New York, NY 10021
(212) 752-0813

American Society of Interior Designers
National Headquarters
1430 Broadway
New York, NY 10018
(212) 944-9220

New York Chapter
200 Lexington Avenue
New York, NY 10016
(212) 685-3480

American Society of Magazine Photographers, Inc.
419 Park Avenue South, #1407
New York, NY 10016
(212) 889-9144

Art Directors Club of New York
250 Park Avenue South
New York, NY 10003
(212) 674-0500

Association of American Publishers
220 East 23rd Street
New York, NY 10010
(212) 689-8920

Association of the Graphic Arts
5 Penn Plaza
New York, NY 10001
(212) 279-2100

The Children's Book Council, Inc.
PO Box 709
New York, NY 10276
(212) 254-2666

CLIO
336 East 59th Street
New York, NY 10022
(212) 593-1900

Foundation for the Community of Artists
280 Broadway, Suite 412
New York, NY 10007
(212) 227-3770

Graphic Artists Guild
11 West 20th Street
New York, NY 10011
(212) 463-7730

Guild of Book Workers
521 Fifth Avenue
New York, NY 10175
(212) 757-6454

Institute of Outdoor Advertising
342 Madison Avenue
New York, NY 10173
(212) 986-5920

International Advertising Association, Inc.
342 Madison Avenue, Suite 2000
New York, NY 10173
(212) 557-1133

The One Club
3 West 18th Street
New York, NY 10011
(212) 255-7070

The Public Relations Society of America, Inc.
33 Irving Place
New York, NY 10003
(212) 995-2230

Society of American Graphic Artists
32 Union Square, Room 1214
New York, NY 10003
(212) 260-5706

Society of Illustrators
128 East 63rd Street
New York, NY 10021
(212) 838-2560

Society of Photographers and Artists Representatives
1123 Broadway
New York, NY 10010
(212) 924-6023

continued on page 441

Pat Foster
Artists Representative
6 East 36 Street
Suite #1R
New York, New York 10016
(212) 685-4580
FAX on request

Representing:
Dru Blair
Illustrator

Sandra Freeman
Represents
3333 Elm Street Suite 105
Dallas, Texas 75226
(214) 871-1956 • FAX: (214) 748-2133

Representing :
Karla Tuma Cooper
(214) 495-7762

"I Have A Good Eye."

Sandra Freeman Represents
3333 Elm Street Suite 105
Dallas, Texas 75226
(214) 871-1956 • FAX: (214) 748-2133

Representing:
Jennifer Harris
(214) 750-4669

**Sandra Freeman
Represents**
3333 Elm Street Suite 105
Dallas, Texas 75226
(214) 871-1956 • FAX: (214) 748-2133

Representing:
Mary Haverfield
(214) 520-2548

Horn in the night...

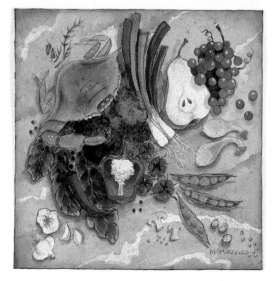

Sandra Freeman Represents
3333 Elm Street Suite 105
Dallas, Texas 75226
(214) 871-1956
FAX: (214) 748-2133

Representing:
Rusty Jones
(214) 306-3835

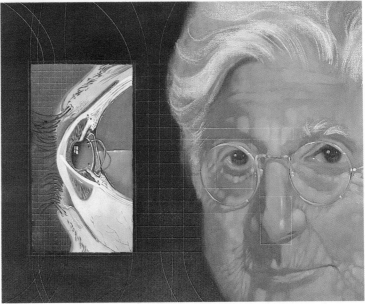

**Sandra Freeman
Represents**
3333 Elm Street Suite 105
Dallas, Texas 75226
(214) 871-1956 • FAX: (214) 748-2133

Representing:
Lynn Rowe Reed
(214) 635-9587

continued from page 434

Society of Publication Designers
60 East 42nd Street, Suite 1130
New York, NY 10165
(212) 983-8585

Television Bureau of Advertising
477 Madison Avenue
New York, NY 10022
(212) 486-1111

Type Directors Club of New York
60 East 42nd Street, Suite 1130
New York, NY 10165
(212) 983-6042

U.S. Trademark Association
6 East 45th Street
New York, NY 10017
(212) 986-5880

Volunteer Lawyers for the Arts
1285 Avenue of the Americas
New York, NY 10019
(212) 977-9270

Women in the Arts
325 Spring Street, Room 200
New York, NY 10013
(212) 691-0988

OHIO

Advertising Club of Cincinnati
PO Box 43252
Cincinnati, OH 45243
(513) 575-9331

Cleveland Society of Communicating Arts
Maggie Moore
PO Box 14759
Cleveland, OH 44114
(216) 621-5139

Columbus Society of Communicating Arts
c/o Orby Kelly
1900 Crown Park Court
Columbus, OH 43220
(614) 761-9405

Design Collective
D.F. Cooke
131 North High Street
Columbus, OH 43215
(614) 464-2883

PENNSYLVANIA

Art Directors Club of Philadelphia
2017 Walnut Street
Philadelphia, PA 19103
(215) 569-3650

TEXAS

Advertising Club of Fort Worth
1801 Oak Knoll
Colleyville, TX 76034
(817) 283-3615

Art Directors Club of Houston
PO Box 271137
Houston, TX 77277
(713) 661-7267

Dallas Society of Visual Communications
3530 High Mesa Drive
Dallas, TX 75234
(214) 241-2017

Print Production Association of Dallas/Fort Worth
PO Box 160605
Irving, TX 75016

VIRGINIA

Industrial Designers Society of America
Walker Road, Suite 1142-E
Great Falls, VA 22066
(703) 759-0100

National Association of Schools of Art and Design
11250 Roger Bacon Drive
Reston, VA 22090
(703) 437-0700

Tidewater Society of Communicating Arts
PO Box 153
Norfolk, VA 23501

WASHINGTON

Allied Arts of Seattle, Inc.
107 South Main Street
Seattle, WA 98104
(206) 624-0432

Seattle Ad Federation
c/o Margaret Oliver
PO Box 4159
Seattle, WA 98104
(206) 623-8307

Seattle Design Association
PO Box 1097
Main Office Station
Seattle, WA 98111
(206) 285-6725

Society of Professional Graphic Artists
c/o Steve Chin, President
85 South Washington Street, Suite 204
Seattle, WA 98104

WISCONSIN

Coalition of Women's Art Organizations
123 East Beutel Road
Port Washington, WI 53074
(414) 284-4458

Illustrators & Designers of Milwaukee
c/o IDM
5600 West Brown Deer Road
Browndeer, WI 53223
(414) 355-1405

Milwaukee Advertising Club
231 West Wisconsin Avenue
Milwaukee, WI 53203
(414) 271-7351

Dennis Godfrey
95 Horatio Street
New York, New York 10014
(212) 807-0840

Representing:
Jeffrey Adams
David Stimson

JEFFREY ADAMS

DAVID STIMSON

Dennis Godfrey
95 Horatio Street, Suite 203
New York, New York 10014
(212) 807-0840
FAX (818) 577-6025
In San Francisco:
Corey Graham
(415) 956-4750

Representing:
Joel Nakamura

■ GODFREY

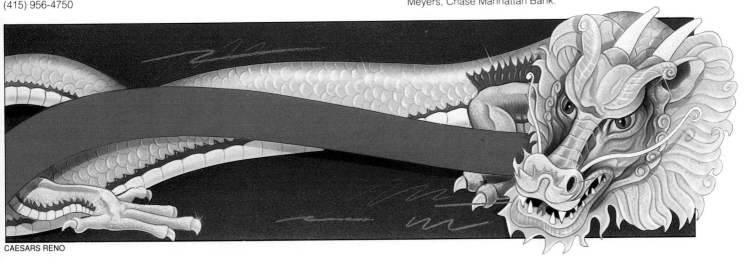

CAESARS RENO

SY DEVORES

DECORATE IT

COKE

David Goldman Agency
41 Union Square West
Suite 918
New York, New York 10003
(212) 807-6627 • FAX: (212) 463-8175

Representing:
Norm Bendell

Yes, we have an animation reel!

David Goldman Agency
41 Union Square West
Suite 918
New York, New York 10003
(212) 807-6627 • FAX: (212) 463-8175

Representing:
Norm Bendell

Yes, we have an animation reel!

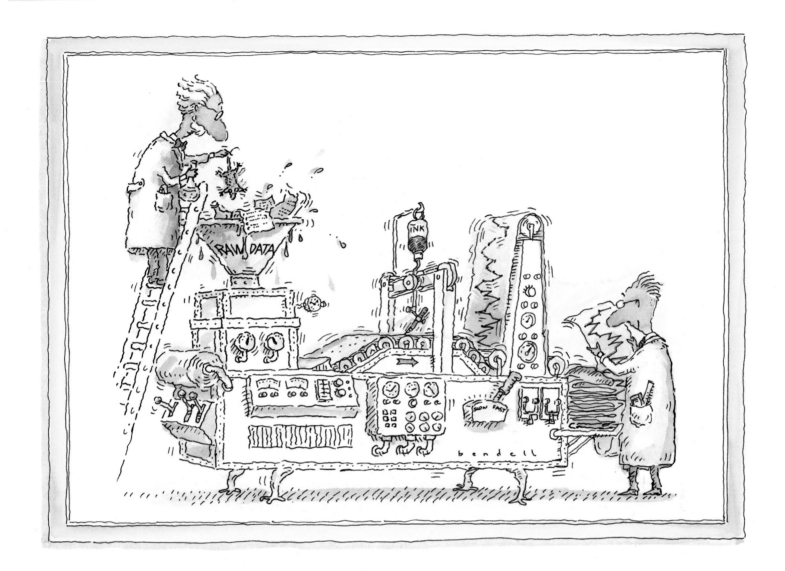

David Goldman Agency
41 Union Square West
Suite 918
New York, New York 10003
(212) 807-6627 • FAX: (212) 463-8175

Representing:
Keith Bendis

"Cutting The Risks"   New Republic

"Taking The Big Bath"   Fortune Magazine

"Pre-emptive Strike"   New York Times Magazine

David Goldman Agency
41 Union Square West
Suite 918
New York, New York 10003
(212) 807-6627 • FAX: (212) 463-8175

Representing:
Keith Bendis

"Dream Vacation"   Philadelphia Magazine

David Goldman Agency
41 Union Square West
Suite 918
New York, New York 10003
(212) 807-6627 • FAX: (212) 463-8175

Representing:
Mitchell Rigié

David Goldman Agency
41 Union Square West
Suite 918
New York, New York 10003
(212) 807-6627 • FAX: (212) 463-8175

Representing:
Mitchell Rigié

David Goldman Agency
41 Union Square West
Suite 918
New York, New York 10003
(212) 807-6627 • FAX: (212) 463-8175

Representing:
James Yang

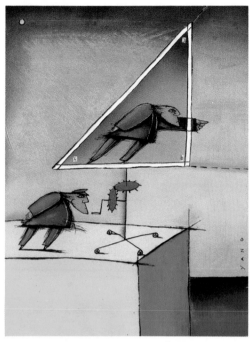

Lotus Magazine

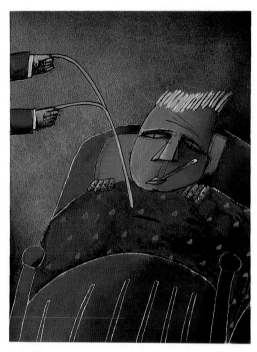

East West Magazine

Republic New York Corporation Annual Report 1988

Spector, Knapp & Baughman, Ltd.

David Goldman Agency
41 Union Square West
Suite 918
New York, New York 10003
(212) 807-6627 • FAX: (212) 463-8175

Representing:
James Yang

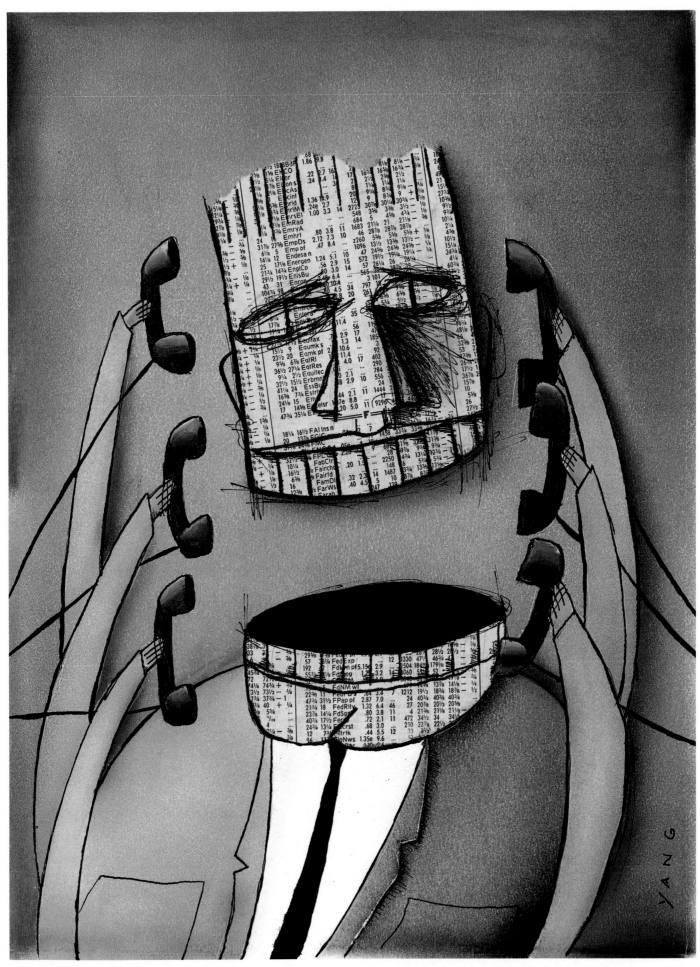

Gwen Goldstein
91 Hundreds Road
Wellesley Hills, Massachusetts 02181
(617) 235-8658

Represents:
Cathy Diefendorf

Gwen Goldstein
91 Hundreds Road
Wellesley Hills, Massachusetts 02181
(617) 235-8658

Represents:
Lane Gregory

Gwen Goldstein
91 Hundreds Road
Wellesley Hills, Massachusetts 02181
(6l7) 235-8658

Represents:
Susan Spellman

454

WHERE ADVERTISING COMES FROM

This is probably going to sound familiar.

The account team and the client hammer out a strategy.

The account team gives the strategy to creative to do creative.

They give it to media to do a media plan.

And later they give it to research to test it and see if it worked. (I told you it was going to sound familiar).

That's how most advertising agencies work. And it works pretty well.

So why change it?

At Della Femina, McNamee WCRS, Boston I think we've stumbled onto something that works better. It's called "The Brand Team" and it's pretty much based on the premise that if two heads are better than one, then eight heads are better than two.

No, it's not a committee, it's a team. And it works like this:

For every major project people are assigned from creative, account services, media, research and production (The Brand Team). Everyone is involved right from the beginning. Everyone is thinking about the project from their own discipline. And believe me, a good idea (not necessarily an ad but an advertising idea) is as likely to come from media as it is from creative or production. After a few meetings there's a wonderful camaraderie among the players. Everyone's on track. Everyone feels ownership. And I think the creative product benefits from it.

Production is on line ahead of time thinking about ways of getting it done. The marketing people are setting up the client as to where we're going so nobody's blindsided. And let's face it, when you run in a pack, some of you are going to get through. The Brand Team will help sell creative.

The advertising agency business brings together the most diverse groups of people I know. And if you can get everyone talking the same line, it's very powerful.

The creative product is better for it and with all that support you've definitely got a better chance of selling it.

Ron Lawner
Creative Director
Della Femina, McNamee WCRS, Inc.
Boston, Massachusetts

**Barbara Gordon
Associates**
165 East 32nd Street
New York, New York 10016
(212) 686-3514

Representing:
Glenn Harrington

Barbara Gordon
Associates Ltd.
165 East 32 Street
New York, N.Y. 10016
212-686-3514

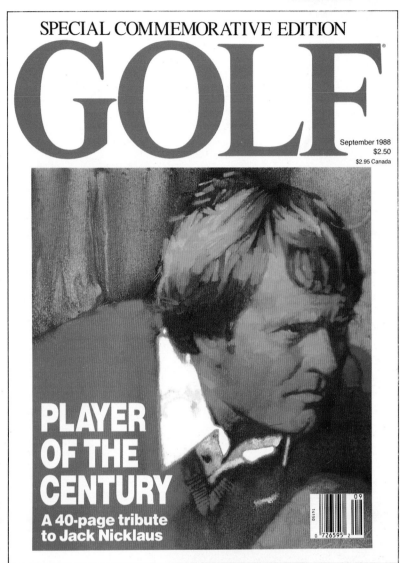

SPECIAL COMMEMORATIVE EDITION

GOLF

September 1988
$2.50
$2.95 Canada

PLAYER OF THE CENTURY

A 40-page tribute to Jack Nicklaus

Barbara Gordon Associates
165 East 32nd Street
New York, New York 10016
(212) 686-3514

Representing:
Jim Dietz

Barbara Gordon
Associates Ltd.
165 East 32 Street
New York, N.Y. 10016
212-686-3514

**Barbara Gordon
Associates**
165 East 32nd Street
New York, New York 10016
(212) 686-3514

Representing:
Jackie Jasper

Clients: Alcott & Andrews, ABC, Avon
Books, Bantam Books, Barney's,
Geoffrey Beene, Bergdorf Goodman,
Bloomingdales, Burberry's, Burlington
Industries, Coach Bags, Cosmopolitan,
Doubleday, Good Housekeeping, Hanes
Hosiery, Hearst Pub., Hess Oil, Hickey
Freeman, Nabisco, Republic Bank.

**Barbara Gordon
Associates**
165 East 32nd Street
New York, New York 10016
(212) 686-3514

Representing:
Nenad Jakesevic
Sonja Lamut

Artists also have a large selection of
stock artwork available.

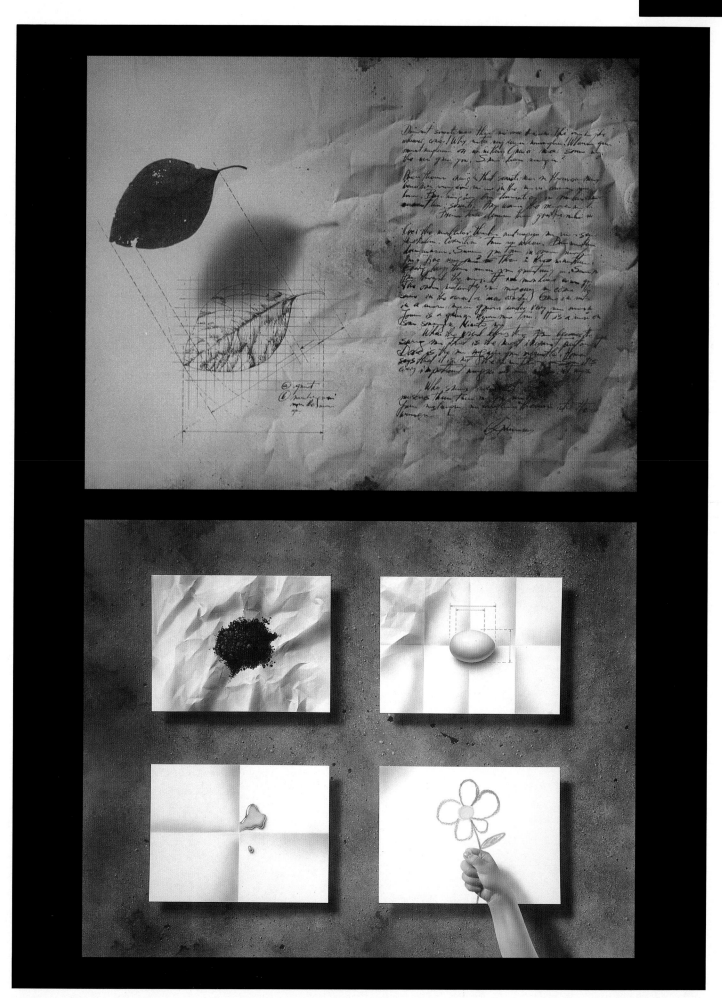

**Barbara Gordon
Associates**
165 East 32nd Street
New York, New York 10016
(212) 686-3514

Representing:
**Nenad Jakesevic
Sonja Lamut**

Artists also have a large selection of
stock artwork available.

Barbara Gordon
Associates Ltd.
165 East 32 Street
New York, N.Y. 10016
212-686-3514

**Barbara Gordon
Associates**
165 East 32nd Street
New York, New York 10016
(212) 686-3514

Representing:
Liz Kenyon

Illustrations ©1989 Liz Kenyon

Anita Grien
155 East 38th Street
New York, New York 10016
(212) 697-6170 • FAX (212) 697-6177

Representing:
Alex "Mangal" Zwarenstein
Fanny Mellet Berry
Jerry McDaniel • Hal Just

ALEX "MANGAL" ZWARENSTEIN

FANNY MELLET BERRY

JERRY MCDANIEL   ILLUSTRATION & COMPUTER ART

HAL JUST

464

Anita Grien
155 East 38th Street
New York, New York 10016
(212) 697-6170 • FAX (212) 697-6177

Representing:
Ellen Rixford • Alan Reingold
Don Morrison • Dolores Bego

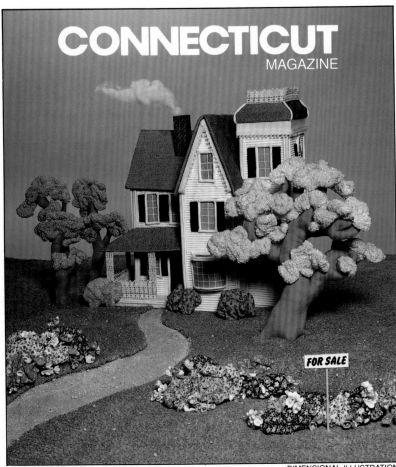

ELLEN RIXFORD   DIMENSIONAL ILLUSTRATION

ALAN REINGOLD

DON MORRISON

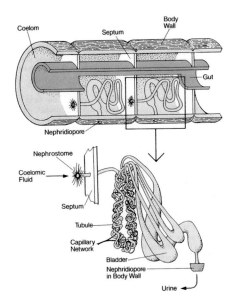

Figure 35-8   EXCRETORY ORGANS IN INSECTS.
In insects, excretory products in the coelomic fluid pass through the walls of the many Malpighian tubules (arrows), and urine is discharged into the hindgut where it is eliminated with the solid fecal waste.

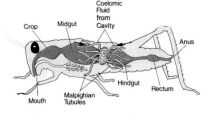

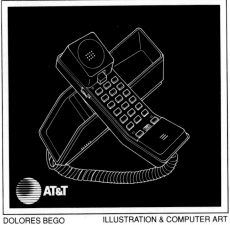

DOLORES BEGO   ILLUSTRATION & COMPUTER ART

458 Newtown Turnpike
Weston, Connecticut 06883
Telephone (203) 454-4687
Fax (203) 227-1366
Contact
Harriet Kasak

Carolyn Croll

Eldon Doty

PORTFOLIO

458 Newtown Turnpike
Weston, Connecticut 06883
Telephone (203) 454-4687
Fax (203) 227-1366
Contact
Harriet Kasak

**Randy
Chewning**

**Randy
Verougstraete**

ARTISTS' REPRESENTATIVE

HK
PORTFOLIO

Scott Hull Associates
68 East Franklin Street
Dayton, Ohio 45459
(513) 433-8383
(212) 966-3604 NYC
(513) 433-0434 FAX

M A R K   B R A U G H T

Scott Hull Associates
68 East Franklin Street
Dayton, Ohio 45459
(513) 433-8383
(212) 966-3604 NYC
(513) 433-0434 FAX

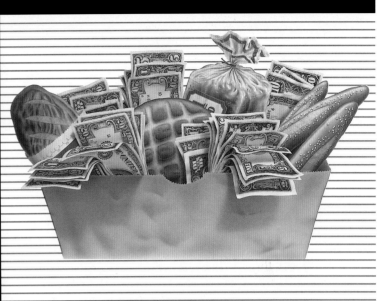

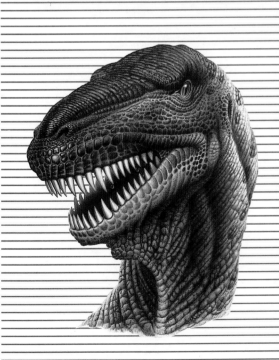

Scott Hull Associates
68 East Franklin Street
Dayton, Ohio 45459
(513) 433-8383
(212) 966-3604 NYC
(513) 433-0434 FAX

J O H N   B U X T O N

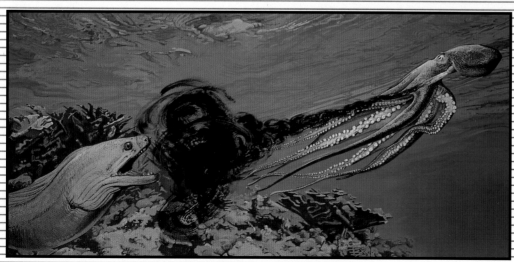

Scott Hull Associates
68 East Franklin Street
Dayton, Ohio 45459
(513) 433-8383
(212) 966-3604 NYC
(513) 433-0434 FAX

GREG DEARTH

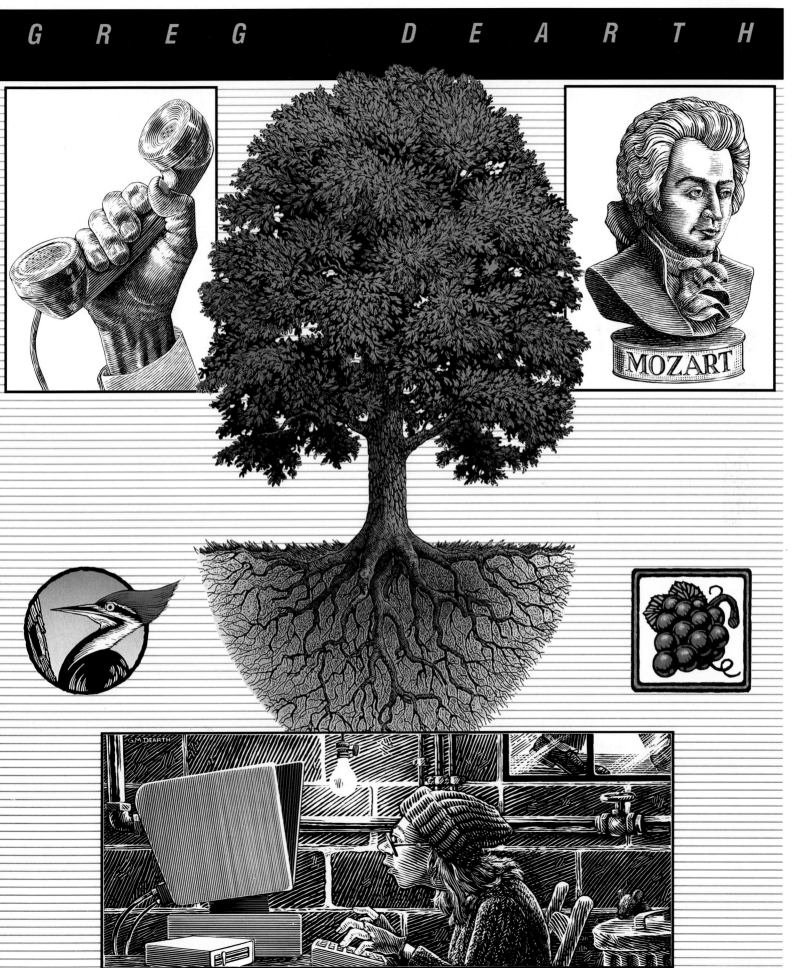

Scott Hull Associates
68 East Franklin Street
Dayton, Ohio 45459
(513) 433-8383
(212) 966-3604 NYC
(513) 433-0434 FAX

D A V I D   G R O F F

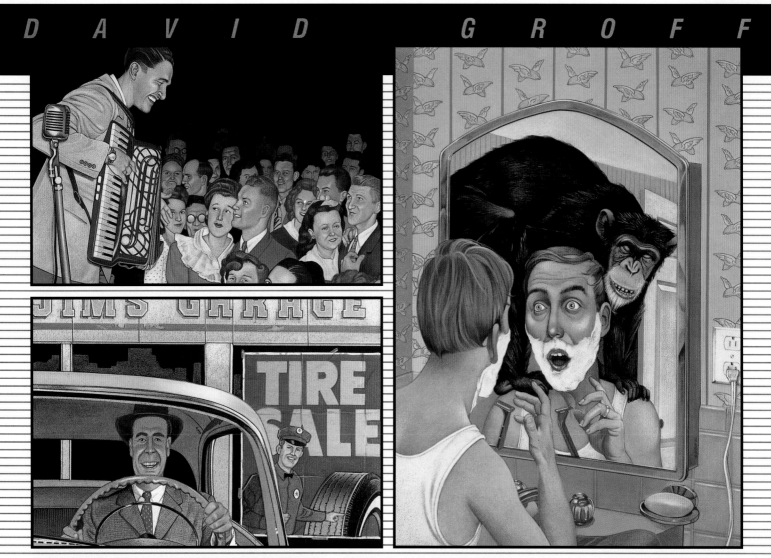

Scott Hull Associates

68 East Franklin Street
Dayton, Ohio 45459
(513) 433-8383
(212) 966-3604 NYC
(513) 433-0434 FAX

B I L L   J A M E S

Scott Hull Associates
68 East Franklin Street
Dayton, Ohio 45459
(513) 433-8383
(212) 966-3604 NYC
(513) 433-0434 FAX

GREG LaFEVER

Scott Hull Associates
68 East Franklin Street
Dayton, Ohio 45459
(513) 433-8383
(212) 966-3604 NYC
(513) 433-0434 FAX

DON VANDERBEEK

Scott Hull Associates
68 East Franklin Street
Dayton, Ohio 45459
(513) 433-8383
(212) 966-3604 NYC
(513) 433-0434 FAX

JOHN MAGGARD

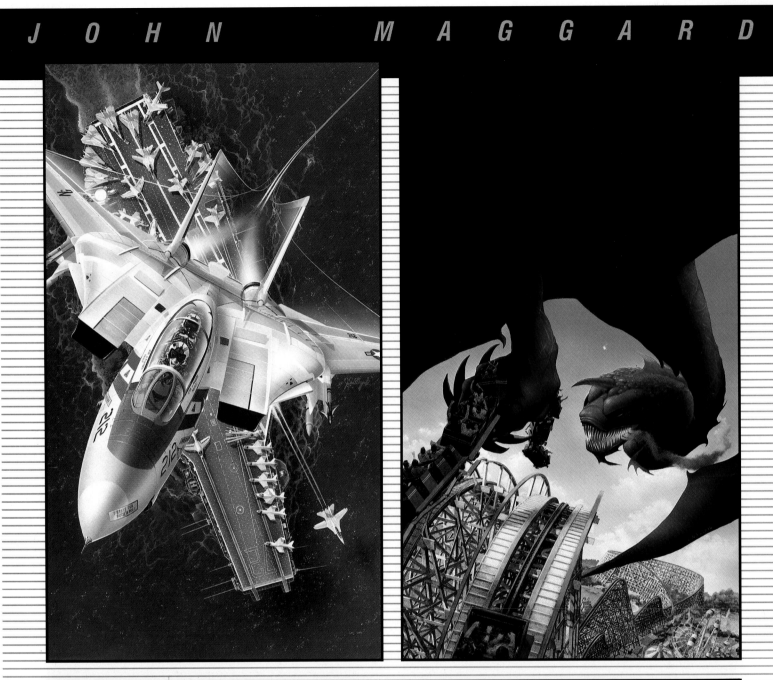

Scott Hull Associates
68 East Franklin Street
Dayton, Ohio 45459
(513) 433-8383
(212) 966-3604 NYC
(513) 433-0434 FAX

T E D P I T T S

Scott Hull Associates
68 East Franklin Street
Dayton, Ohio 45459
(513) 433-8383
(212) 966-3604 NYC
(513) 433-0434 FAX

Represented in Chicago by
Sell, Inc.
(312) 565-2701

GREG MANCHESS

Scott Hull Associates
68 East Franklin Street
Dayton, Ohio 45459
(513) 433-8383
(212) 966-3604 NYC
(513) 433-0434 FAX

M A R K   R I E D Y

Scott Hull Associates
68 East Franklin Street
Dayton, Ohio 45459
(513) 433-8383
(212) 966-3604 NYC
(513) 433-0434 FAX

DON VANDERBEEK

Scott Hull Associates
68 East Franklin Street
Dayton, Ohio 45459
(513) 433-8383
(212) 966-3604 NYC
(513) 433-0434 FAX

L E E   W O O L E R Y

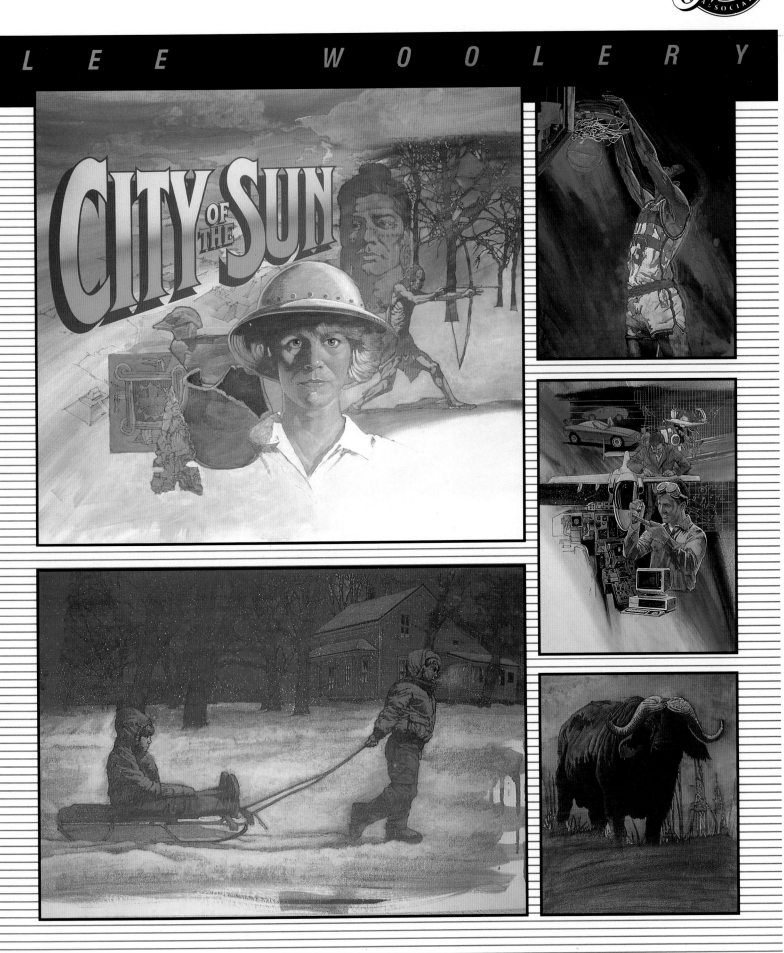

Clare Jett & Associates
21 Theater Square Suite 200
Louisville, Kentucky 40202
(502) 561-0737
FAX: (502) 585-4551

ROY
Wiemann

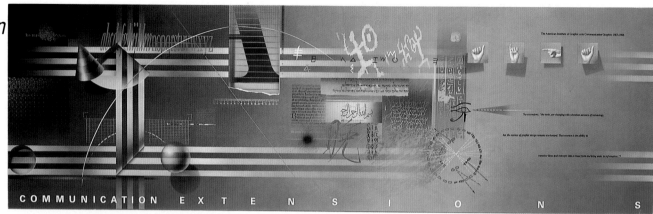

PAUL
Wolf

For additional work, see illustration section.

ANNETTE
Cable

MARK
Cable

482

Clare Jett & Associates
21 Theater Square Suite 200
Louisville, Kentucky 40202
(502) 561-0737
FAX: (502) 585-4551

CYNTHIA
Torp

For additional work, see illustration section.

JOHN
Mattos

For additional work, see illustration section.

DAVID
Wariner

MARK
Cable

Please phone for complete portfolios.
(502) 561-0737

Tania Kimche
470 West 23rd Street
New York, New York 10011
(212) 242-6367

Representing:
E.T. Steadman

T A N I A
TANIA KIMCHE ARTISTS REPRESENTATIVE 470 West 23rd St., NY. NY. 10011
(212) 242-6367

FLORIDA CREATIVE ADV.

BANTAM BOOKS

ELIAS BASEBALL BOOKS

IBM/HDM ADV.

Tania Kimche
470 West 23rd Street
New York, New York 10011
(212) 242-6367

Representing:
Rafál Olbínski

CITYTRUST BANCORP ANNUAL REPORT

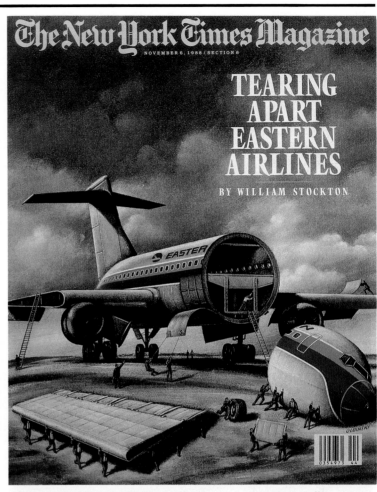

PLAYBOY

BUSINESS WEEK

INC. MAGAZINE

485

Tania Kimche
470 West 23rd Street
New York, New York 10011
(212) 242-6367

Representing:
Richard A. Goldberg
(in Greater New York Area)

Boston/New England Rep.
Deborah Lipman
(617) 451-6528
(508) 877-8830

Other regions:
(617) 338-6369

IBM/MCM ADV.

SOFT LOGIC INC.

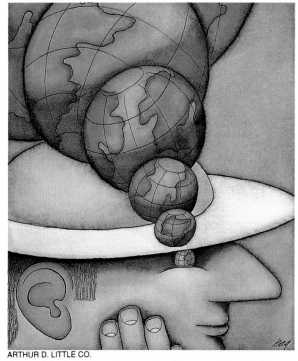

ARTHUR D. LITTLE CO.

STATE STREET BANK

Tania Kimche
470 West 23rd Street
New York, New York 10011
(212) 242-6367

Representing:
Christopher Zacharow

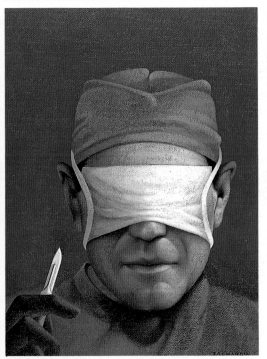

DISCOVER MAGAZINE

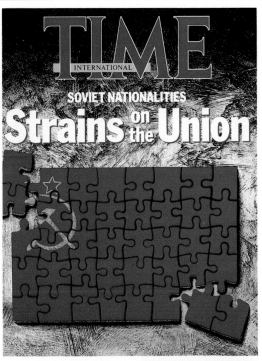

DOUBLEDAY BOOKS

PERSONAL FINANCE QUARTERLY

PROVIDENT NATIONAL BANK

FRITO-LAY

PACIFIC TELESIS

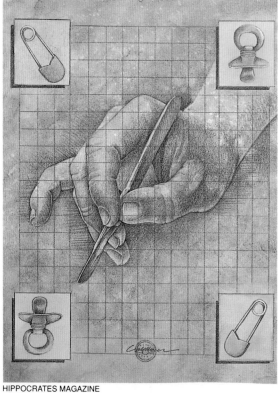

HIPPOCRATES MAGAZINE

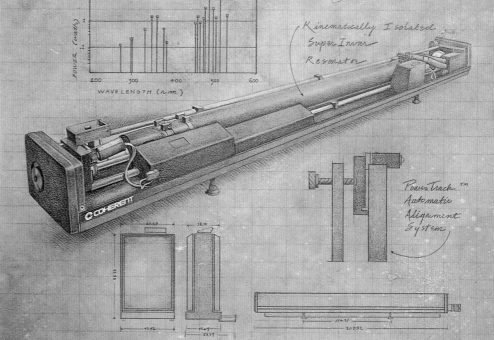

COHERENT, INC.

Tania Kimche
470 West 23rd Street
New York, New York 10011
(212) 242-6367

Representing:
Hom & Hom
(In all regions except Los Angeles)

Los Angeles Rep:
The Repertory
Loretta Greer
Robert Jacobs
(213) 931-7449

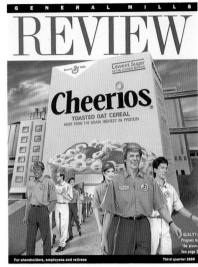

GENERAL MILLS

THE PROMOTION GROUP

STEIDL/YOUNGER DESIGN

Tania Kimche
470 West 23rd Street
New York, New York 10011
(212) 242-6367

Representing:
M. Schottland

Washington DC Area:
M. Schottland
(202) 328-3825

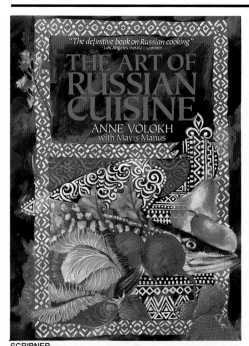

SCRIBNER

FALCON ADV.

WORLD BUSINESS MAGAZINE

NASA

H O W   T O   S E L L   B R E A K - T H R O U G H   A D V E R T I S I N G

The only way to sell breakthrough advertising is by doing breakthrough work. If that's all the client ever sees throughout your myriad of presentations, eventually they'll buy something good.

But, when the fresh ideas stop coming on a campaign as a result of many rejections, beg off. Press the creative director to put someone else on the account. This happens all the time, and it's better to move onto something new. We've all gotten burned out after dozens of layouts and storyboards. I generally threaten to quit and, depending on your seniority, this strategy can work.

A case comes to mind of a recent retail account I was assigned to (the client shall remain nameless). I found out after a year that there's a limit to how many ways I can say, BUY ONE. GET ONE FREE. After accusing the account team of turning me into a hack, I was politely excused from that particular piece of business.

Breakthrough work doesn't always require a breakthrough strategy, but it helps. The more you know about what you're advertising, the more focused you will be. That's why creative people should not let terms like 'demographics' and 'user friendly' frighten them. The information is there to assist you. If you already know it, at least pretend you're listening when the account team debriefs the client.

I spent a year studying acting in New York early in my career, not because I wanted to be an actor, but because doesn't every profession require you to be a salesman?

So, you've got a good strategy. The client hasn't seen any work yet, so they still like you. Now the time comes to conceive. Personally, I do my best not to pick up a copy of CA, The One Show Book, or the D & AD Annual for inspiration until at least the second day. It's a bad habit we all get into, and can often spurn ideas that resemble previously traversed territory. Where can you look for

inspiration outside of your head?

• Books (not about advertising). These are always a good place to start. I spend at least a day, early in the development of a campaign, in the best bookstore I can find. I pore through all kinds of subjects until the owner pressures me to start buying. Then I charge them to the project.

• Movies. The video rental store is a whole new kind of research library. Rental fees also apply to the project.

• Magazines (preferably those where you don't understand the language). Look at photographs, type design, anything that stretches the boundaries of conventional advertising layouts. Personally, if I see Garamond typeface one more time, condensed or otherwise, I think I'll scream.

• Your mother. Don't be afraid to bounce ideas off anyone willing to listen. In my case, it generally ends up being my mother, rather than another art director. I figure she's the consumer.

• Copywriters. Something else I'm open to is letting the writer art direct while I write. Who ever remembers who came up with which idea? In the long run it's irrelevant, because everyone ends up taking the credit anyway.

So, now you've come up with a campaign that's going to win a gold pencil in The One Show. How do you sell it? At Chiat/Day/Mojo, it's more difficult to get the idea out of the agency than it is to sell it to the client. Is it the best ad it can be? Now you can open up CA, The One Show, or D & AD and compare notes.

When the day comes to present your campaign to the client, it is important that you show at least three great ideas. If you've only got one after two weeks' work, then run with it. But remember, if you project to the client that they're going to think you've gone too far, they will.

No matter how off the wall your concept may be, keep referring to its relevance to the research. That helps. Also, make sure the layouts and storyboards are rough. If you can, draw them yourself. If not, find a storyboard artist and try to teach him or her how not to draw...the looser the better. I often swipe photos in frames to help the client visualize the concept.

continued on page 504

491

Kirchoff/Wohlberg, Inc.
866 United Nations Plaza
New York, New York 10017
(212) 644-2020

ROBERT STEELE

RAE ECKLUND

J. BRIAN PINKNEY

DARA GOLDMAN

TOM LEONARD

CAROL NICKLAUS

Kirchoff/Wohlberg, Inc.

866 United Nations Plaza
New York, New York 10017
(212) 644-2020

MARYJANE BEGIN CALLANAN

ARIEH ZELDICH

DONALD COOK

DON MADDEN

FLOYD COOPER

DORA LEDER

Bill and Maurine Klimt
15 West 72nd Street
New York, New York 10023
(212) 799-2231

Representing:
Frank Morris

Chicago: (312) 565-2701 Dan Sell
Dallas: (214) 521-5156 Linda Smith
Los Angeles: (818) 995-6883 Tony
Yamada

Bill and Maurine Klimt
15 West 72nd Street
New York, New York 10023
(212) 799-2231

Representing:
Brian Kotzky
Doug Gray

BRIAN KOTZKY

DOUG GRAY

BRIAN KOTZKY

DOUG GRAY

Bill and Maurine Klimt
15 West 72nd Street
New York, New York 10023
(212) 799-2231

Representing:
Gary Penca
Jaime de Jesus

GARY PENCA

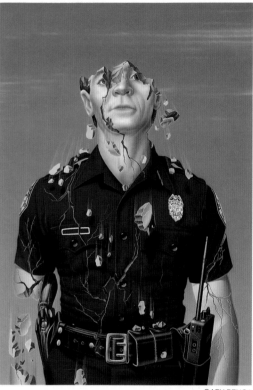

GARY PENCA

JAIME DE JESUS

JAIME DE JESUS

Bill and Maurine Klimt
15 West 72nd Street
New York, New York 10023
(212) 799-2231

Representing:
Wil Cormier

KLIMT

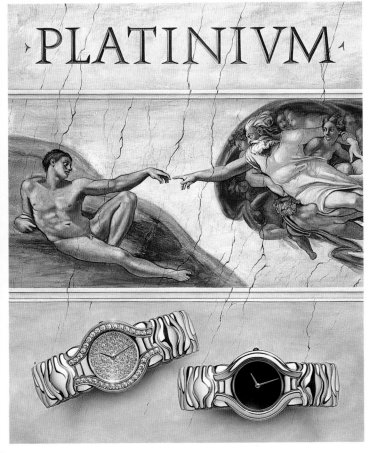

Bill and Maurine Klimt
15 West 72nd Street
New York, New York 10023
(212) 799-2231

Representing:
Mark Skolsky
Carla Sormanti

MARK SKOLSKY

MARK SKOLSKY

CARLA SORMANTI

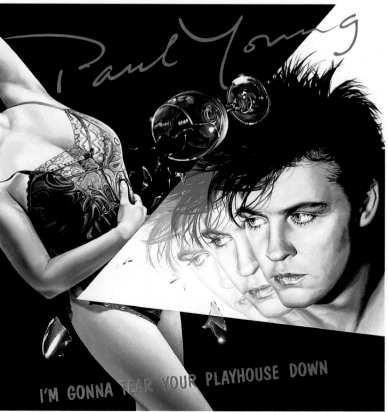

CARLA SORMANTI

498

Bill and Maurine Klimt
15 West 72nd Street
New York, New York 10023
(212) 799-2231

Representing:
Alan Neider

Represented in Connecticut and
Massachusetts by:
John Brewster/Creative Services
126 Old Redding Road
West Redding, Connecticut 06896
(203) 226-4724 • FAX: (203) 454-9904

Sandy Kline
637 Hawthorne
Houston, Texas 77006
(713) 522-1862

Representing
Mike Robins
(713) 669-1629

Sandy Kline
637 Hawthorne
Houston, Texas 77006
(713) 522-1862

Representing
Keith Graves
(512) 478-3338

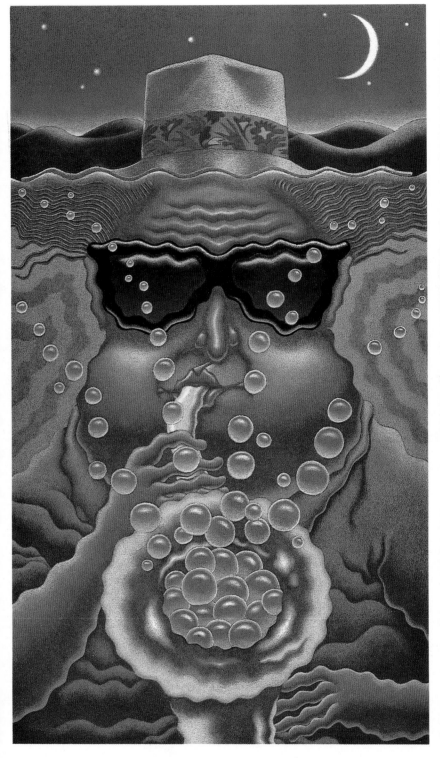

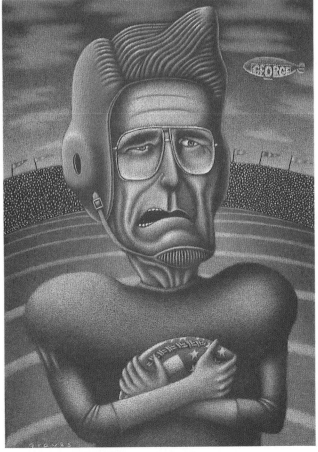

Cliff Knecht
309 Walnut Road
Pittsburgh, Pennsylvania 15202
(412) 761-5666

Representing:
Jim Trusilo

Also see Showcase Volume 12
pps. 458-461

Cliff Knecht
309 Walnut Road
Pittsburgh, Pennsylvania 15202
(412) 761-5666

Representing:
Phil Wilson

Also see Showcase Volume 12
pps. 458-461

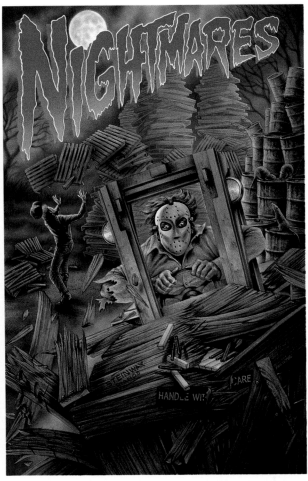

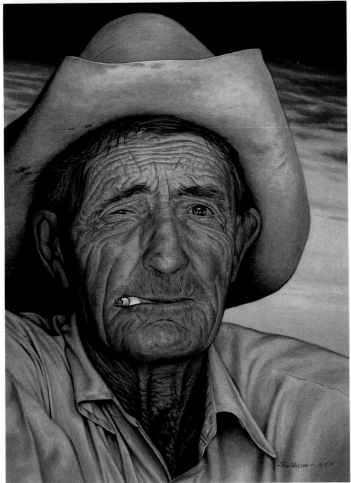

continued from page 491

The same goes for TV. If your idea requires moving images and you can swipe those from movies, TV, MTV, wherever, do it. Assemble a video storyboard, lay down some music—anything to get your idea across.

If the client is still having difficulty, ask if you can expose some consumers to the concept. They rarely say no to this suggestion—how can they? I find the consumer is usually much smarter than the client when it comes to taking chances.

You've sold the idea! Now you have to execute it. Look to hire photographers and illustrators outside their given area of expertise. Some of my best fashion work has been done by photojournalists or still life photographers. Keep an open mind.

All of this is about challenging yourself and the medium of advertising. Because if it's not fresh, if we've seen it before, if you know you're going to hate it when it's done—why bother?

Michael Smith
Art Director
Chiat/Day/Mojo Inc. Advertising
Venice, California

Kolea
Artist's Repesentative
Pier 70
2815 Alaskan Way, Suite 37-A
Seattle, Washington 98121
(206) 443-0326

Clients Include:
Zellerbach Paper Company,
Weyerhaeuser, Microsoft, Black Angus
Restaurants, Weisfield Jewelers,
Nalleys, Seafirst Bank, U.S. National
Track Cycling Association, NIntendo,
Nu-Day Diet Plan, KISW-FM 100,
Columbia Winery, Chateau Ste.
Michelle Winery.

Glenn Yoshiyama • Calligraphy & Letter Design

Kolea
Artist's Representative
Pier 70
2815 Alaskan Way, Suite 37-A
Seattle, Washington 98121
(206) 443-0326

Clients Include:
Motorola, Microsoft Corporation, Longevity Magazine, Penthouse Magazine, Playboy, Washington Energy Co., Epson Emerica, Doubleday Books, Devon Systems, First Union National Bank,

Philadelphia Magazine, Coldwell Banker, Capitol Bancorp, Intel Corporation, Cascade Microtek, Home Capitol, Porton Products, Lotus Magazine, Agega World Magazine.

Kolea

George Abe ◆ Acrylic

Kolea
Artist's Representative
Pier 70
2815 Alaskan Way, Suite 37-A
Seattle, Washington 98121
(206) 443-0326

Kolea

Don Baker • Graphic & Computer

Kolea
Artist's Representative
Pier 70
2815 Alaskan Way, Suite 37-A
Seattle, Washington 98121
(206) 443-0326

Clients Include:
Westlake Center; Century Square;
Nordstrom; Let's Talk Magazine;
Columbia Winery; Seal Press; Group
Health; Valley Medical Center, Seattle;
City Light; Herman Miller Office
Furniture; US West Communications;
A.E.I.; Kasala; Interchecks, Inc.

Kolea

Elaine Cohen ♦ Pastel

Kolea

Philip Howe • Mixed Medium

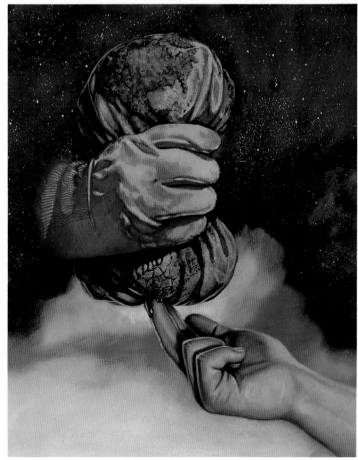

Kolea
Artist's Representative
Pier 70
2815 Alaskan Way, Suite 37-A
Seattle, Washington 98121
(206) 443-0326

Clients Include:
Washington Magazine, Alaska Airlines
Magazine, World Magazine,
The Weekly, Technical Analysis of
Stocks and Commodities, Wilkens
and Peterson, Unix Magazine.

Kolea

Jere Smith • Acrylic

Jere Smith • Acrylic

Kolea
Artist's Representive
Pier 70
2815 Alaskan Way, Suite 37-A
Seattle, Washington 98121
(206) 443-0326

Clients Include:
Chateau Ste. Michelle Winery; San Juan Winery; Seal Press; GTE; Pacific First Federal Bank; Interchecks, Inc.; Creative Education Inc.; Alaska Airlines; Unix Magazine; Seattle Childrens Theatre; Pacific Northwest Magazine; Washington Natural Gas; American Savings Bank; Washington State Apple Commission; Superior Farms; Tacoma Orthopedic Surgeons Association.

Kris Wiltse • Watercolor

511

**Pamela Korn
& Associates**
321 East 12th Street
New York, New York 10003
(212) 529-6389
FAX: (212) 529-6375

Representing:
Wendy Braun

Partial Client List Includes:
Backer Spielvogel Bates • Miller
Brewing Co. • Lotus • Food & Wine
Travel & Leisure • Audio • New York
Times • Boston Globe Magazine
Philadelphia Magazine • Chicago
Magazine • L.A. Times • Sunday
London Observer • Psychology Today

Personal Computing • Success
Whittle Communications • Random
House
Awards & Sourcebooks:
Communication Arts • Graphis
Photo/Design • American Showcase
#11, 12 • Graphic Artist Guild
Directory #5 • JCA Annual

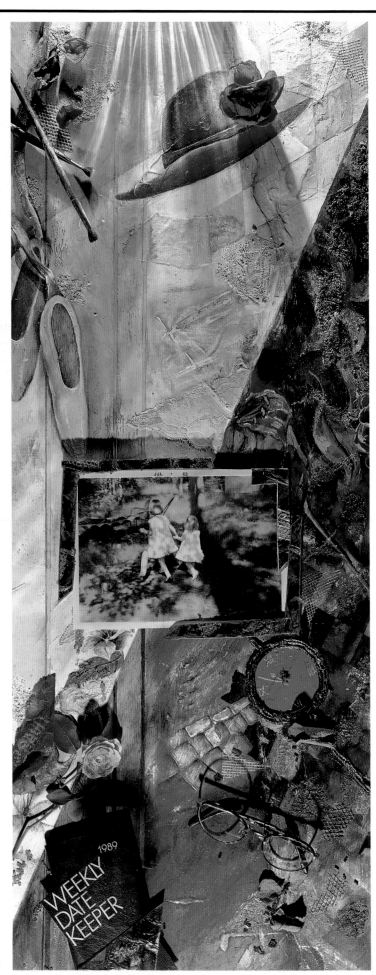

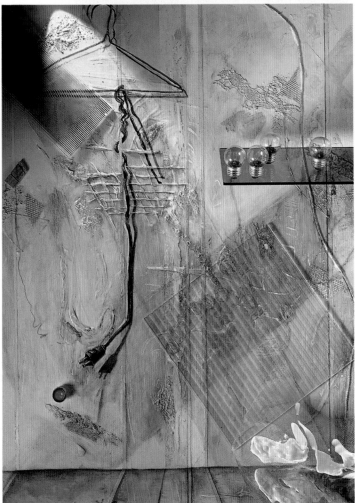

Pamela Korn & Associates
321 East 12th Street
New York, New York 10003
(212) 529-6389
FAX: (212) 529-6375

Representing:
Brian Ajhar

Partial Client List Includes:
Bozell, Jacobs, Kenyon & Eckhardt •
DDB Needham • FCB/Leber Katz
Partners • J. Walter Thompson • Scali,
McCabe, Sloves • Wells, Rich, Greene •
General Foods • General Electric •
Maxwell House • McDonalds • Forbes •
Newsweek • Sports Illustrated •

Rolling Stone • Time
Awards & Sourcebooks:
American Illustration • Communication
Arts • Graphis • How Magazine • Print •
Society of Illustrators Annual • Humor
#1, 2 • JCA Annual • American
Showcase# 9, 10, 11, 12 • Black Book
1988 • Graphic Artist Guild Directory #5

**Pamela Korn
& Associates**
321 East 12th Street
New York, New York 10003
(212) 529-6389
FAX (212) 529-6375

Representing:
Jeff Moores

Partial Client List Includes:
BBDO • DDB Needham • Lord
Einstein O'Neil • W.B. Doner & Co.
AT&T • American Express • Chubb
Insurance • Home Box Office
International Olympic Committee
Saab • Seagrams • Forbes
Business Week • McGraw Hill

Money Magazine • New York
Magazine • New York Times • Self
Whittle Communications
Awards & Sourcebooks:
Communication Arts • Print • Society
of Illustrators Humor # 1, 2 • Art
Direction • American Showcase #11,12
Graphic Artist Guild Directory # 5

Pamela Korn
& Associates
321 East 12th Street
New York, New York 10003
(212) 529-6389
FAX: (212) 529-6375

Representing:
Kurt Vargö

Partial Client List Includes: DDB
Needham Worldwide • Ogilvy & Mather
Direct • Saatchi & Saatchi DFS Compton
• Harold Cabot & Co • DCA Advertising •
CBS Records • AT&T • Delta Airlines •
Federal Express • Forbes • Newsweek •
Time • Whittle Communications • Broom
& Broom • Corporate Annual Reports

Awards & Sourcebooks: Print Magazine
May/June 1989 Feature Article •
American Illustration • Prints Regional
Design • Society of Illustrators New
Illustration • Adweek Portfolios Volume
#10, 11, 1986 & 1989
School of Visual Arts, Media Arts Faculty
Member

KURT VARGO

VARGO

IS RETAIL BAD FOR YOUR IMAGE?

Stop me if this has ever happened to you. You try to convince a marketing director or ad manager who has already closed off the list of agencies to include your agency. "You're not the type of agency we're looking for..." he says. You respond, "we do alot of retail-type advertising...aren't you interested in selling your products?" His response, "of course, but we need to build our image and frankly you're not an image agency."

My true story was for a pitch to the folks who invented Teddy Ruxpin, the talking teddy bear. They also created Laser Tag, the "bang, you're dead! toy" of the eighties using infrared light shot from pistols. Worlds of Wonder was the name of the company and their next venture was into the world of inter-active video. I couldn't convince the senior marketing people that despite selling hamburgers for McDonald's, cars for Toyota, or Ralphs groceries or tickets to amusement parks like Knott's Berry Farm or Marine World Africa USA, that Davis, Ball & Colombatto (formerly DJMC) could also sell, or more importantly, attract purchasers for their new inter-active video. It seems our heavy mix of retail-type clients suggested to the folks at WOW that we couldn't sell their products as well as a packaged goods or brand-type agency. What happened? Well, they hired the other type of agency and like all the rest of the products from WOW, they folded. Belly-up! Their stock when last reported traded at something like .17 cents a share, if that, down from $33.00.

Should they have demanded a little more from their advertising? Like the objective to sell their products? I believe so. And so should most clients. For our entire history we've been labeled as a retail agency, like the term suggests we don't care about good creative or that all we debate over in creative meetings is logo size and how big the prices should be.

In fact, we do argue about those things but only after we agree that the concept is both original and zap-proof.

That it will momentarily paralyze the viewers' forefingers preventing that ultimate form of criticism, zapping, from happening.

But, we also work the concept over and over to assure ourselves that it sells the product with such appeal and conviction that viewers become consumers and respond not within weeks, but hours. Agencies that steep themselves with retail clients and grow, have to come to think in terms of minutes, hours and days versus weeks, months and years. Our clients' businesses demand advertising that gets their business moving immediately; not long-term or over time. Sure those are nice residual effects of the advertising, but clients usually worry about today's sales or this weekend's numbers versus that proverbial five year plan. After all, most clients are just as worried about losing their jobs for lack of performance as agencies are about losing the account, for the same reason.

Retail is not an ugly word if you're in the business to sell something. Nor does it have to imply ugly looking ads or commercials. At DBC, the two co-exist quite nicely...to such an extent that we proudly point to our Clio winning retail approach for Borateem Bleach, or our international homerun in creating the "Mac Tonight" campaign for McDonald's, and more. Combining an intrusive creative approach with a hard-selling, "buy it today" approach has helped us dramatically, and of course, more to the point— our clients. If we're accused of creating advertising that makes people buy things, terrific. So before you rule out certain client possibilities because you're worried that their retail needs will limit your creative potential and hurt your image or reel, don't!

There's plenty of creativity in making cash registers ring.

Brad A. Ball
President
Davis, Ball & Colombatto Advertising
Los Angeles, California

Jane Lander Associates
33 East 30th Street
New York, New York 10016
(212) 679-1358

Representing:
Frank Riley
(201) 423-2659

Member Joint Ethics Committee,
Member Society of Illustrators

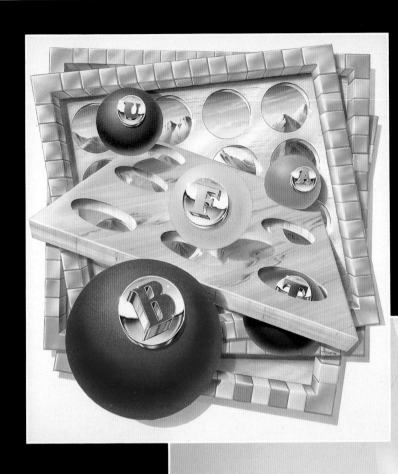

Peter and George Lott
60 East 42nd Street
New York, New York 10165
(212) 953-7088

Member: Art Directors Club
Society of Illustrators

Represent:
Wendell McClintock

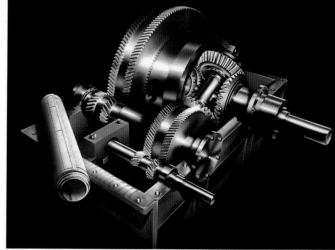

Peter and George Lott
60 East 42nd Street
New York, New York 10165
(212) 953-7088

Member: Art Directors Club
Society of Illustrators

Represent:
Tim O'Brien

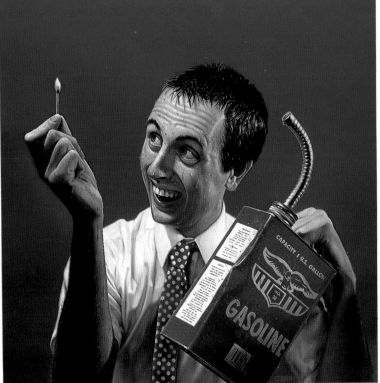

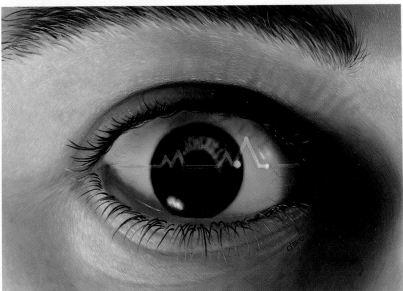

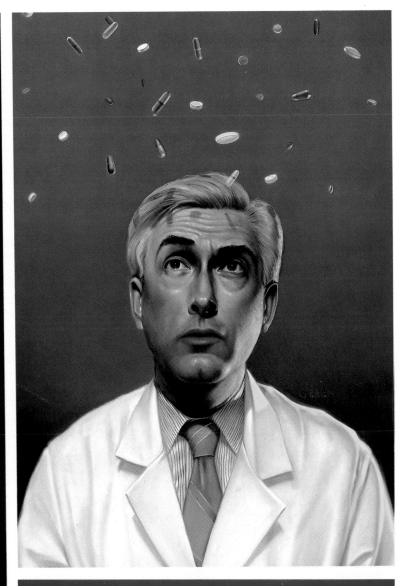

BUY WAR BONDS and STAMPS

Be an ARTIST!
$5, $10, $15 FOR ONE DRAWING

RITA MARIE AND FRIENDS

SERVING QUALITY ART · coast·to·coast

ILLUSTRATION

DAVID BECK
MORT DRUCKER
JIM ENDICOTT
MARLA FRAZEE
KEN GOLDAMMER
RICK GONNELLA
ROBERT GUNN
HARUO ISHIOKA

GARY PIERAZZI
BOB PRYOR
PAUL ROGERS
GARY RUDDELL
DICK SAKAHARA
DANNY SMYTHE
MARK SPARACIO
GREG WRAY

PHOTOGRAPHY

BRUCE AYRES   TIM SCHULTZ

Rita Marie & Friends
Rita Marie
(213) 934-3395 • FAX: (213) 936-2757
Rodney Ray
(312) 222-0337 • FAX: (312) 883-0375

Representing:
Paul Rogers

Rita Marie & Friends
Rita Marie
(213) 934-3395 • FAX: (213) 936-2757
Rodney Ray
(312) 222-0337 • FAX: (312) 883-0375

Representing:
Paul Rogers

Rita Marie & Friends
Rita Marie
(213) 934-3395 • FAX: (213) 936-2757
Rodney Ray
(312) 222-0337 • FAX: (312) 883-0375

Representing:
Rick Farrell

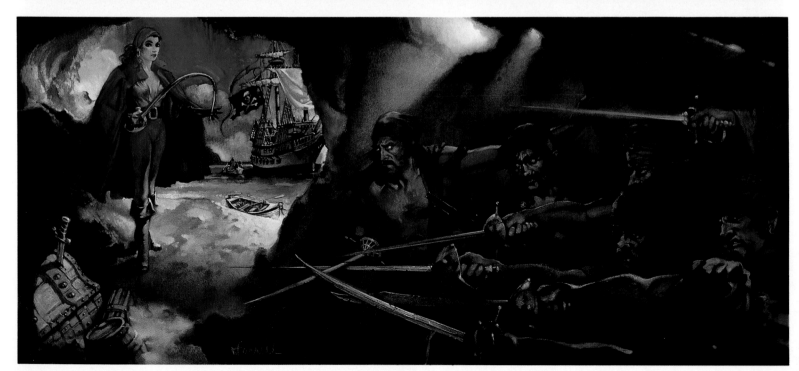

Rita Marie & Friends
Rita Marie
(213) 934-3395 • FAX: (213) 936-2757
Rodney Ray
(312) 222-0337 • FAX: (312) 883-0375

Representing:
Greg Wray

Rita Marie & Friends
Rita Marie
(213) 934-3395 • FAX: (213) 936-2757
Rodney Ray
(312) 222-0337 • FAX: (312) 883-0375

Representing:
Mark & Erin Sparacio
(516) 579-6679

Rita Marie & Friends
Rita Marie
(213) 934-3395 • FAX: (213) 936-2757
Rodney Ray
(312) 222-0337 • FAX: (312) 883-0375

Representing:
Dick Sakahara
28826 Cedarbluff Drive
Rancho Palos Verdes, California 90274
(213) 541-8187 • FAX: (213) 541-9217

Tokyo Representative:
Jonn Uomoto & Associates
7-21-17 Tono Estate, Suite 803
Minatoku, Tokyo 106, Japan
Tel: 03-479-6476
FAX: 03-479-6477

Pamela Neail Associates
27 Bleecker Street
New York, New York 10012
(212) 673-1600
FAX: (212) 673-7687

Represents:
Linda Richards

GATOR-AID

Pamela Neail Associates
27 Bleecker Street
New York, New York 10012
(212) 673-1600
FAX: (212) 673-7687

Represents:
Linda Richards

Pamela Neail Associates
27 Bleecker Street
New York, New York 10012
(212) 673-1600
FAX: (212) 673-7687

Representing:
Peter McCaffrey

Pamela Neail Associates
27 Bleecker Street
New York, New York 10012
(212) 673-1600
FAX: (212) 673-7687

Represents:
Celeste Henriquez

PAMELA
NEAIL

Pamela Neail Associates
27 Bleecker Street
New York, New York 10012
(212) 673-1600
FAX: (212) 673-7687

Represents:
Michele Laporte

PAMELA
NEAIL

Pamela Neail Associates
27 Bleecker Street
New York, New York 10012
(212) 673-1600
FAX: (212) 673-7687

Represents:
Marina Levikova

PAMELA
NEAIL

Pamela Neail Associates
27 Bleecker Street
New York, New York 10012
(212) 673-1600
FAX: (212) 673-7687

Represents:
Jenny Vainisi

PAMELA
NEAIL

Pamela Neail Associates
27 Bleecker Street
New York, New York 10012
(212) 673-1600
FAX: (212) 673-7687

Represents:
Gaylord Welker

PAMELA
NEAIL

The Neis Group
11440 Oak Drive
Shelbyville, Michigan 49344
(616) 672-5756
FAX: (616) 672-5757

GARY ELDRIDGE

JUDY NEIS
(616) 672-5756
FAX
(616) 672-5757

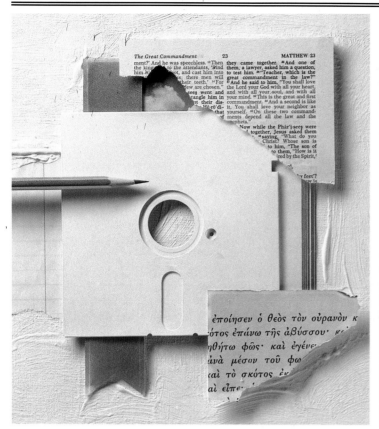

LIZ CONRAD

JUDY NEIS
(616) 672-5756
FAX
(616) 672-5757

The Neis Group
11440 Oak Drive
Shelbyville, Michigan 49344
(616) 672-5756
FAX: (616) 672-5757

TOM BOOKWALTER

JUDY NEIS
(616) 672-5756
FAX
(616) 672-5757

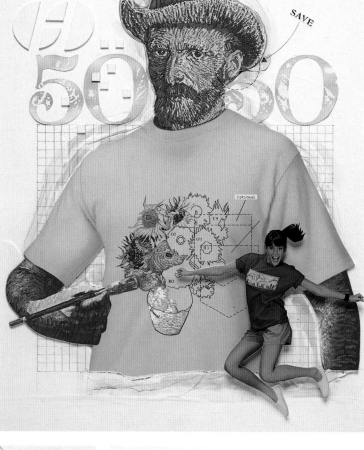

Clients

Amana
American Airlines
Amway
Anheuser Busch
Archway
AT&T
Beech Craft
California Cooler
Carnation
Caterpillar
Chicago Tribune
Coleco
Coleman
Coors
Domino's
Dow Corning
Doubleday
DuPont
Exxon
Frito Lay
Gerber
Hanes
Herman Miller
Honeywell
Illinois Bell
John Deere
Kellogg's
Kraft
L.O.F.
Maytag
M&M Mars
McDonald's
Mead Paper
Merrill Lynch
Michigan Bell
Miles Laboratories
Miller Brewing
N.F.L.
National Wildlife
N.J. Lottery
Phillip Morris
Ray-O-Vac
Republic Airlines
Rockwell Inter'l
Six Flags
Stroh's
State of Michigan
3M
Tonka
Toyota
Tropicana
Turtle Wax
United Technologies
Upjohn
Volvo
Walmart
Washington Post
Winnebago

The Organisation
New York Office:
267 Wyckoff Street
Brooklyn, New York 11217
(718) 624-1906
Contact: Pauline Mason

London Office:
69 Caledonian Road
London N1 9BT
Tel. 01 833 8268
01 278 5176, 01 833 4161
FAX: 01 833 8269
Contact: Janet Eaton

Also representing Grahame Baker, Enikoe Bakti, Yvonne Chambers, Emma Chichester Clark, Maxwell Lawrence Dorsey, David Eaton, Glyn Goodwin, Neil Gower, Nicholas Hely Hutchinson, Leslie Howell, Alan Morrison, Katherine Mynott, Lawrence Mynott, Alan McGowan, Kevin O'Brien, Michael O'Shaughnessy, Guy Passey, Janet Pontin, Max Schindler, Jayne Simkins, Amanda Ward, Nick Williams.

Extensive brochure available on request.

NATACHA LEDWIDGE ▲ NADINE WICKENDEN ▼   MARK ENTWISLE ▲ MICHAEL FRITH ▼

ZAFER BARAN ▲   PETER GOODFELLOW ▼

RUTH RIVERS ▲ SUSAN HELLARD ▼

**The Penny &
Stermer Group**

A division of:
Barbara Penny Associates, Inc.
48 West 21 Street
New York, New York 10010
(212) 243-4412 • FAX: (212) 627-0832

Representing:
Julia Noonan

Over 15 years of experience in
solving design problems. Works in
a wide range of styles and media.

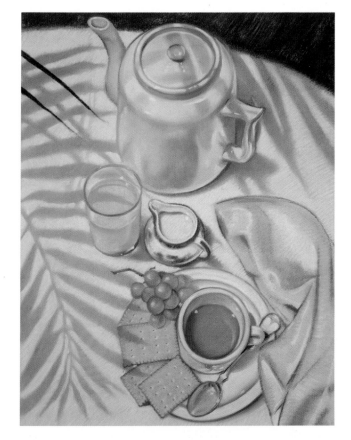

Representing:
Julia Noonan

Schering Corp.

Glenn Foods, Inc.

**The Penny &
Stermer Group**
A division of:
Barbara Penny Associates, Inc.
48 West 21 Street
New York, New York 10010
(212) 243-4412 • FAX: (212) 627-0832

Representing:
Ron Becker

**The Penny &
Stermer Group**
A division of:
Barbara Penny Associates, Inc.
48 West 21 Street
New York, New York 10010
(212) 243-4412 • FAX: (212) 627-0832

Representing:
Thomas Payne

THE
PENNY &
STERMER
GROUP

**The Penny &
Stermer Group**

A division of:
Barbara Penny Associates, Inc.
48 West 21 Street
New York, New York 10010
(212) 243-4412 • FAX: (212) 627-0832

Representing:
Michael Hostovich

© 1989 Michael Hostovich
All rights reserved

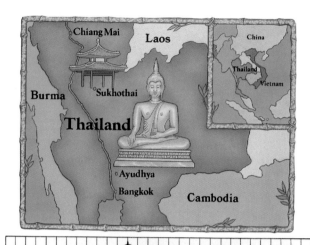

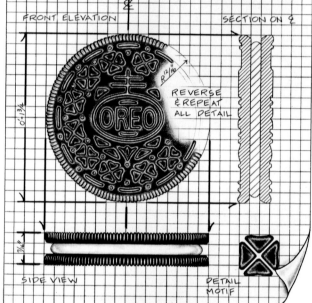

**The Penny &
Stermer Group**
A division of:
Barbara Penny Associates, Inc.
48 West 21 Street
New York, New York 10010
(212) 243-4412 • FAX: (212) 627-0832

Representing:
Terri Starrett

THE
PENNY &
STERMER
GROUP

◆—◆· RUBEN DeAnda ·◆—◆

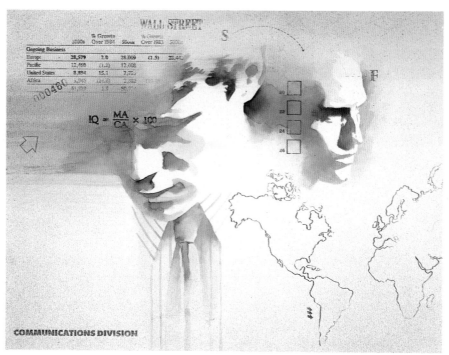

·Denise Hilton-Putnam·

RICHARD · W · SALZMAN

ARTIST · REPRESENTATIVE

6 1 9 · 2 7 2 · 8 1 4 7
FAX / 6 1 9 · 2 7 2 · 0 1 8 0

NY / 212 · 997 · 0115   SF / 415 · 751 · 7935   LA / 213 · 276 · 4298

TO VIEW ADDITIONAL WORK SEE SHOWCASE 9, 10, 11, 12; WORKBOOK 8, 9, 10, 11, 12; THE CREATIVE ILLUSTRATION BOOK 1

·DOUG BOWLES·

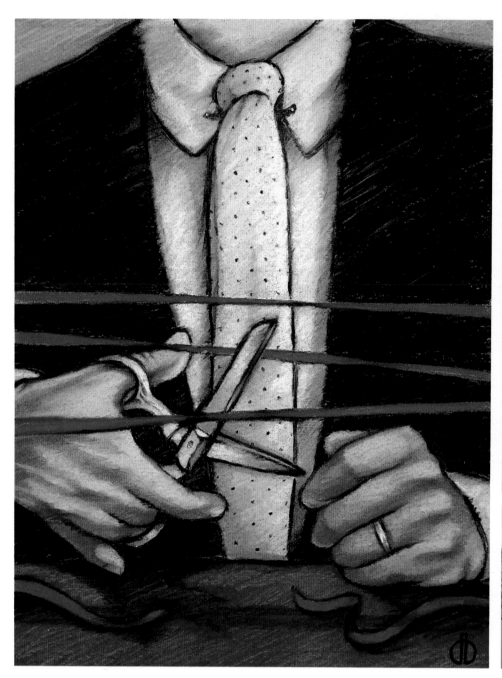

·CHRIS McALLISTER·

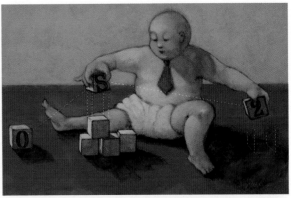

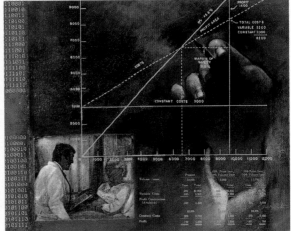

Fran Seigel
515 Madison Avenue
New York, New York 10022
(212) 486-9644

Representing:
Kinuko Y. Craft

KINUKO Y. CRAFT

NYNEX/YOUNG & RUBICAM

SIMON & SCHUSTER

ASSOCIATED AVIATION UNDERWRITERS

CRABTREE & EVELYN

Fran Seigel
515 Madison Avenue
New York, New York 10022
(212) 486-9644

Representing:
Earl Keleny

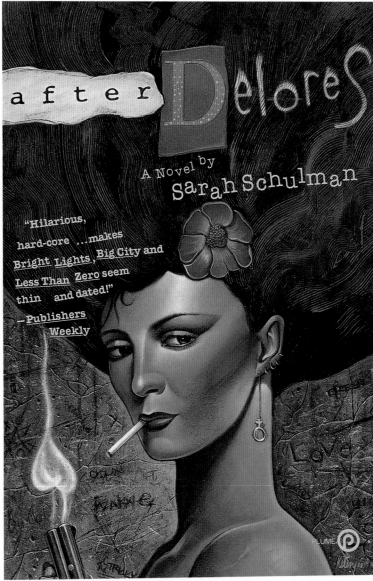

NEW AMERICAN LIBRARY

NORTHWESTERN MUTUAL LIFE INSURANCE

NORTHWESTERN MUTUAL LIFE INSURANCE

ATLANTIC RECORDS

Fran Seigel
515 Madison Avenue
New York, New York 10022
(212) 486-9644

Representing:
Larry McEntire

TEXAS MONTHLY (A.D. KATHY MARCUS)

ARKANSAS TIMES (A.D. CHRIS KIESLER)

WORLD MONITOR (A.D. GREG PAUL)

YANKEE MAGAZINE (A.D. JAY PORTER)

PSYCHOLOGY TODAY (A.D. REGINA JONES)

Fran Seigel
515 Madison Avenue
New York, New York 10022
(212) 486-9644

Representing:
Catherine Deeter

U.S. FOREST SERVICE

ODESSEY HOUSE

HARCOURT BRACE JOVANOVICH

Fran Seigel
515 Madison Avenue
New York, New York 10022
(212) 486-9644

Representing:
Mirko Ilic

It's my "mistake!"

Mirko Ilić

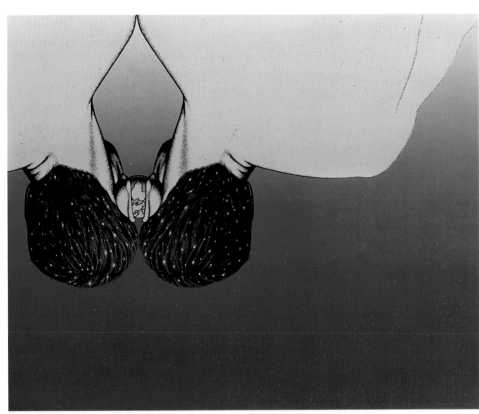

PENTAGRAM DESIGN/DREXEL BURNHAM LAMBERT

TIME MAGAZINE (EXXON OIL SPILL)

FEAR AND LOATHING ON THE AIRLINE TRAIL

I awoke one Friday morning to the telephone blaring at 5 a.m.

"Hey, Phil. Sorry to wake you, but could you come in early today? We've got a crunch job on a full page newspaper ad."

I told the production coordinator that I'd get there as quickly as I could.

The agency I was working for was one of the larger Houston advertising firms. I'd been there just about a year and I'd been in the business just about a year.

A client of ours had to get an ad into the weekend Atlanta paper. We had all the materials, but had to make a noontime flight to get the ad counter-to-counter to beat the deadline. One hitch: the copy was still getting the final run-through in the client's legal department. As time dragged on, we decided to typeset the copy that we did have and I'd knife the changes as required.

"When will the typesetter have the copy output?"

"About 10:30. Maybe 11:00."

"When am I supposed to paste this thing together and get it to the airport? The flight is at noon."

The Intercontinental Airport in Houston is a terrific airport, don't get me wrong. Well, at least it's not O'Hare. But everyone in Houston is at least 45 minutes away from the airport. It doesn't matter where you live in town. I've got one friend who's a scant six miles away and it still takes him 45 minutes.

We decided that I'd get the ad together as best as possible, blue line everything else on the board, and paste up the ad on the airplane. Not just fly-by-night advertising, but production-by-flight advertising. A new service for the agency repetoire. I taped the keyline securely to a lap board, affixed a t-square down the side to keep things square, and took along a large triangle to do my type alignment. Remember, this was a full page newspaper ad, so you can imagine what the mess looked like.

Racing down to the typesetter, I grabbed the copy and a duplicate for making corrections as soon as it came out of the soup and passed through the wax. I think I broke every speed limit in Texas to get to the airport 24 miles away. Yes, it took me 45 minutes. Getting there, I found no parking spots around the terminal. I mean none. My flight was departing in minutes. I shot into an opening under an entry ramp that had just about four inches of clearance above my car. I bet myself that it wouldn't be here when I got back, but I couldn't worry about that now. I bolted for the gate.

I made the plane just as they were preparing to close the door. Stowing the board and type for take-off, I relaxed in the first First Class seat I'd ever been in. I'd argued that if I was to have enough room to put together an ad in flight, I'd have to go First Class. Once up to altitude, I pulled out the board and feverishly worked on cramming the reams of copy into the ad. The gentleman in the seat next to me was concerned as to what I was doing, especially since it was to the exclusion of food, drink, and all the other trappings of First Class.

"I've got to get this ad together for an afternoon deadline at the paper", I told him without so much as a glance up.

He ordered the second of four Bloody Marys that he would have on that two hour flight.

The ad was done ten minutes before touchdown in Atlanta. Once down, I rushed out of the airport and grabbed the first available cab. We got to the newspaper five minutes before deadline. My contact came down to meet me at the front desk.

"How was the flight?"

"Fine. I've got the ad here. Can I get to a phone to call to see if there are any corrections or revisions?" I asked.

"Would you like something to drink?"

continued on page 562

A D R I A N   D A Y   ····· E M I L Y   G O R D O N

MINIATURE PORTRAITS IN WATERCOLOR, 1 5/8" DIA.

continued from page 559

Something was definitely up. There was no newspaper person on earth this laid back without a reason. I finally convinced him to get me to a phone. Calling back to the agency, I found out the client's lawyers had decided that there were some legal questions remaining on the copy and that the ad had been killed for now. I sat back and looked at the clock. It was 5:20 p.m. and I was in the process of missing my return flight to Houston.

Thanking the contact for his help and sending the ad over to the client's Atlanta office by messenger, I made one more call—this time, to an old college buddy who lived in town. I told him that there was a dinner and some Cuervo Tequila that needed attention if he weren't tied up.

That was ten years ago. Today, I could have leisurely arranged the entire ad on my Mac, easily inserted copy changes or revisions, then modemed the ad to the Atlanta paper without the fear and loathing on the airline trail theatrics. Technology is such a wonderful thing, but it would have killed this story as surely as our client killed the ad.

At least my car was still where I left it when I got back to the airport. All in all, that's probably the most amazing thing about this entire tale.

Phil Watkins III
Associate Creative Director
Carmichael Lynch
Kansas City, Missouri

Paul Willard Associates
815 North 1st Avenue, Suite 3
Phoenix, Arizona 85003
(602) 257-0097

FAX Machine in office.

Representing:
Curtis Parker

Paul Willard Associates
815 North 1st Avenue, Suite 3
Phoenix, Arizona 85003
(602) 257-0097

FAX Machine in office

Representing:
Matthew Foster

Paul Willard associates
ARTIST'S REPRESENTATIVE

Foster

Paul Willard Associates
815 North 1st Avenue, Suite 3
Phoenix, Arizona 85003
(602) 257-0097

FAX Machine in office.

Representing:
Jack Graham